COMPACT
CYMRU

Smugglers of Wales

Twm Elias and
Dafydd Meirion

The
Smugglers Haunt

REST...

Gwasg Carreg Gwalch

First published in Welsh in 2007
Compact Cymru edition: 2017
© Text:: Twm Elias/Dafydd Meirion
Copyright © by Gwasg Carreg Gwalch 2017.

ISBN: 978-1-84524-259-6

Cover design: Eleri Owen
Map: Alison Davies
Gwasg Carreg Gwalch,
12 Iard yr Orsaf, Llanrwst, Wales LL26 0EH
01492 642031

www.carreg-gwalch.com

Achnowledgements

The publishers wish to acknowledge their gratitude
for these images:
Marian Delyth, p. 89 (Borth-y-gest)
Tony Jones, p. 92, 120
Visit Wales (© Crown copyright (2016)), p. 7, 23, 56,
69, 73, 78, 87, 89, 114

Dedicated to:
Alys, Elin and Catrin
and to Delyth, Gwenllian, Rhiannon, Owain,
Nel and the cats

A Tribute to Dafydd Meirion

When we realised that Dafydd and I had a
mutual interest in the history of smugglers and
that we were both planning to publish
something on the subject, it seemed only
natural to co-operate. This turned out to be a
very easy process – the material bounced back
and forth between us in ping-pong fashion by
means of e-mail and after a certain amount of
revamping, the result was this present volume.

I enjoyed collaborating with Dafydd
immensely. He was good-humoured and full of
fun, enthusiastic and full of ideas to the very
end. Our loss is indeed a great one.

Thanks

My thanks to everyone concerned – there are
too many of you to name individually – for all
the snippets of information concerning
smugglers. A great deal of diffuse material and
anecdotes still remain unharvested. This
volume merely lifts the corner of the lid!

Twm Elias
Plas Tan y Bwlch
December 2016

Contents

Introduction

Numerous tales are told, some going back many hundreds of years, concerning bands of men landing wines, spirits and other illegal goods in the dead of night at some of the most remote beaches and creeks of the Welsh coast.

The questions posed by these stories are numerous: who were these people and why were they prepared to put their lives and freedom in jeopardy in order to avoid paying taxes on such goods? What sort of contraband was smuggled along the Welsh coast? Where did these goods come from and who were the customers? Did the smugglers have a free rein or were the authorities, in the form of the revenue men, giving them a hard time?

With its coastline making up some three-quarters of its border, about 600 miles in all, it is not surprising that there are so many stories about smuggling in Wales. Surprisingly though, smuggling has received very little attention from Welsh historians. Is this perhaps because we have been too respectable to admit to this nefarious trade? Whatever the reasons, it is too exciting a story to be left untold.

Tolls list at New Quay harbour

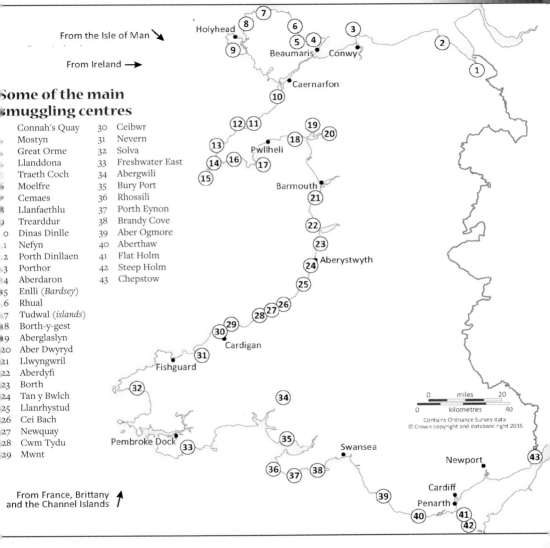

From the Isle of Man

From Ireland

Some of the main smuggling centres

1. Connah's Quay
2. Mostyn
3. Great Orme
4. Llanddona
5. Traeth Coch
6. Moelfre
7. Cemaes
8. Llanfaethlu
9. Trearddur
10. Dinas Dinlle
11. Nefyn
12. Porth Dinllaen
13. Porthor
14. Aberdaron
15. Enlli (*Bardsey*)
16. Rhual
17. Tudwal (*islands*)
18. Borth-y-gest
19. Aberglaslyn
20. Aber Dwyryd
21. Llwyngwril
22. Aberdyfi
23. Borth
24. Tan y Bwlch
25. Llanrhystud
26. Cei Bach
27. Newquay
28. Cwm Tydu
29. Mwnt

30. Ceibwr
31. Nevern
32. Solva
33. Freshwater East
34. Abergwili
35. Bury Port
36. Rhossili
37. Porth Eynon
38. Brandy Cove
39. Aber Ogmore
40. Aberthaw
41. Flat Holm
42. Steep Holm
43. Chepstow

Holyhead
Beaumaris
Conwy
Caernarfon
Pwllheli
Barmouth
Aberystwyth
Cardigan
Fishguard
Pembroke Dock
Swansea
Newport
Cardiff
Penarth

miles 20
kilometres 40
Contains Ordnance Survey data
© Crown copyright and database right 2016

From France, Brittany
and the Channel Islands

The background to smuggling and smugglers

What exactly is a smuggler? The Smuggling Act of 1721 defines a smuggler as anyone who is involved in avoiding the payment of tax on goods, who prevents the revenue department from seizing untaxed goods or who carries arms or acts in secret in the conveyance of such goods. According to Charles Lamb, however, 'He [the smuggler] is the only honest thief.' Lamb maintained that the smuggler had legitimately bought the goods and his only crime was to avoid paying tax on them. At the time, it was a matter of political opinion whether you believed the taxes to be just or not! Adam Smith, the famous eighteenth century economist, described the smuggler as someone who is no doubt highly blameable for violating the laws of his country, is frequently incapable of violating those of natural justice, and who would have been . . . an excellent citizen had not the laws of his country made [smuggling] a crime which Nature never meant to be so.

The word 'to smuggle' comes from the Scandinavian languages. In Danish, 'smug-handle' means illegal goods, in Swedish 'smuga' is a place to hide, and in Icelandic 'smugu' means a hole to creep through.

The levying of taxes on goods has been going on for centuries, and likewise the history of those who have attempted to avoid paying them. Over 2,000 years ago, it is said that Carthage, one of the main trading centres of the ancient world, raised taxes on certain goods but had difficulty in collecting them because of those who tried to avoid payment. During their occupation of the island of Britain, the Romans also faced similar problems, and the Saxon Ethelred, who lived almost a thousand years ago, charged up to a penny, a substantial amount of money in those far off days, on ships and boats landing at Billingsgate. From Ethelred's time to Cromwell's interregnum, it was the king or queen of England who would be the recipient of these taxes. However, from that time onwards payments would find their way to the ever deepening pockets of the government of the day.

A major source of contraband during

1. Tenby; 2. Conwy quay.

the Tudor period were goods which had been seized and landed secretly by pirates. The landing of such goods in Wales (the 'wild west') was fairly easy with Tenby and Milford Haven amongst the most important centres of piracy during that period. At Cardiff, the revenue inspector was in cahoots with the famous pirate John Callis, whilst in Ceredigion, Sir John Perrot took full advantage of this trade as did the pirate/trader Nicholas Hookes in Aberconwy. The difference between a smuggler and a pirate was that the smuggler purchased his goods whilst the pirate would have stolen them. Both classes of criminal, and it was sometimes difficult to differentiate between them, landed their goods without paying tax on them.

In the early seventeenth century, during the turbulent period after the Tudors had severed all links with the Catholic Church, even people became a commodity to be smuggled. These were Catholic priests being smuggled in from Holland to Britain, including two Welshmen; John Roberts of Trawsfynydd and John Jones of Clynnog who were subsequently arrested and executed at Tyburn, London, in 1610. During the twentieth century, both men were beatified by the Catholic Church. It is also said that Welsh Bibles, which had been printed in Dublin, were smuggled into Wales during this period.

But goods were also smuggled out of Britain. For example, the export of wool from England was prohibited during the reign of Edward I in order to establish a domestic weaving industry. Later, in 1276, exports were permitted but a tax of three pence in the pound had to be paid, which amounted to a sixth of the total value of the wool. Consequently, the producers started to export wool illegally from eastern England and the gangs involved were known as 'owlers' – presumably because, like owls. they would be out and about during the hours of darkness. In his endeavours to stop the smuggling of wool, Edward I ordered his fleet to watch the coast from eastern England to south Wales. When the tax on wool was reduced, smuggling decreased until the duty was reimposed in 1660 remaining in place until 1739.

Welsh cattle were smuggled into France. Professor Caroline Skeele, who collected folk tales in Wales during the 1920s, recorded the story of a lad who had helped to shoe cattle in Abergwili Fair and who had in 1809 and 1810 assisted a drover to drive cattle to Kent to be smuggled over to France. This took place during the Napoleonic wars, and it was not just cattle which were being conveyed. There is a story that arms and other goods were also being smuggled to continental Europe.

Towards the end of the seventeenth century, the desire to create and protect industries was not the only factor which led to the levying of substantial taxes on some goods. This was a period which lasted for the next two centuries, when Britain was establishing a world empire. This frequently led to conflict with native people and other European imperial powers and required a powerful navy and army to protect colonial interests. To pay for this, heavy taxes were imposed on imported goods.

However, at that time parliament was dominated by a rich landowning aristocracy who, quite naturally, were not keen simply to tax themselves. They therefore not only introduced or increased taxes on imported luxuries such as spirits, wines, tea, tobacco and spices, but also on

1. The Black Ox Tavern, Abergwili;
2. Chepstow castle above the Wye.

home-produced essential commodities like salt, candles, coal and soap. This caused great hardship to ordinary people as many of these goods were indispensable. Before the days of refrigeration, meat, butter and fish were all preserved over the winter months by being salted.

So burdensome were these taxes, and the laws having been passed in such an undemocratic manner by the parliamentary landowners, that ordinary folk as well as many of the gentry themselves felt it was their moral right not to pay them. It is not surprising, therefore, that the smugglers, who not only challenged the system but also supplied goods at a much cheaper rate, became folk-heroes and received considerable support from all social strata in the community, allowing them to stay one step ahead of the authorities. This was the beginning of the period that can be called the 'golden age of smuggling', which lasted for the next century and a half.

Certainly it was much easier for the government to impose taxes than to collect them. In reality, many of these taxes were both expensive and difficult to collect, and with so many ships and men

fighting overseas, there were insufficient resources back home to prevent the smugglers from bringing un-taxed goods ashore.

In an attempt to collect these taxes on imported goods, the revenue service established customs houses at ports and ships' masters had to report to customs prior to unloading their cargoes so that the relevant taxes could be levied on the goods in question.

However this did not stop the landing of goods secretly elsewhere before reaching the ports. For example, it is said that Bristol merchantmen in the sixteenth century unloaded many of their cargoes in Chepstow and other small ports along the south Wales coast where there were no customs houses. But this was nothing new; since as early as 1387 the mayor of Bristol was ordered to investigate smuggling in the Bristol Channel, and Bristol was the first port to have its own revenue cutter in an endeavour to curb smuggling.

Between 1760 and 1813, taxes were levied on nearly 1,300 different commodities, and this figure would occasionally increase, such as in 1787 when there were 1,425 taxable goods. The tax collecting system was complicated and the tax laws filled six bulky tomes of the Statute Books. Nevertheless, £6 million of taxes were raised annually. However at least another £2 to £3 million 'went unaccounted for' due to smuggling. This implies that official government figures regarding its income are hardly a credible reflection of trade in Britain during this period!

The goods on which tax was levied included wines and spirits, tea, tobacco, spices, soap, lace, silk, linen materials, hats, handkerchiefs, perfume and almanacs. Some Welsh almanacs were published in Dublin and smuggled to Wales, before duty was eventually abolished in 1834.There was even a tax on playing cards, which was not repealed until 1960! Many of these taxes had more of an impact on the poor than on the rich, especially when ordinary goods, such as tea, salt and clothes, were taxed. Tea was very popular by the eighteenth century, and by 1768 a substantial portion of the population drank tea twice a day, with tax having been paid on just a little over a quarter of this amount.

At different periods nearly everyone in Britain benefited from smuggling. Samuel Pepys, who was Secretary to the Admiralty at this time, notes in his diary for

September 1665 that he had bought 37 pounds of cloves and ten pounds of nutmeg in a tavern, knowing full well that they were contraband!

The government was losing substantial revenue due to smuggling. For example, tax was raised on 650,000 pounds of tea in 1743 (tax on tea being levied at a rate of four shillings in the pound), but it is estimated that 1,500,000 pounds of tea was being consumed annually during that period! In 1760, for example, a pound of tea could be bought in Holland for two shillings (10p in today's money), but it cost five times as much to buy in Britain. Tobacco could also be obtained for two shillings a pound on the continent, and yet cost five times as much in Britain. Tax was even higher on brandy. A four gallon tub of French brandy cost fifteen shillings (80p) to buy on the continent, but on being imported to Britain the cost would rise to a staggering £50!

Here are some examples of the tax rates which were levied on various goods: 15 shillings (75p) on a bushel (2,219 cc) of salt, three pence (1.5p) on a pound of candles, seven pence (3p) on a square metre of calico or muslin, three and a half pence (2p) on cotton and linen, a shilling and a penny (6p) on silk, eleven shillings and five pence (57p) on a gallon of French wine, twenty two and six (£1.12) on a gallon of brandy and three shillings and twopence (16p) on a pound of tobacco. 96% of the price of tea was tax!

It is not surprising, therefore, that these taxes were very unpopular, and the impression was that there was a tax on everything. This is how Richard Lloyd of Plas Menai, Caernarfonshire, saw the situation (translation from Welsh verse):

Tax was raised this year ne'er ordained by God
A tax on burying the dead, and a tax on giving birth,
A tax on the water of the river, and a tax on daylight.
And a tax to go to the Hangman's Noose and a tax for being free.

Similarly Sydney Smith observed that there was a tax on 'sauce to improve man's appetite and on drugs to make him better; on the ermine to decorate a judge and on the rope to hang a criminal; on the poor man's salt and the rich man's spice; on the brass nails on the coffin and on the bridesmaid's ribbon.'

Below are listed the amounts of goods seized by the revenue service in 1822-24:

Tobacco	902,684 pounds
Snuff	3,000 pounds
Brandy	135,000 gallons
Rum	253,000 gallons
Gin	227,000 gallons

However as only a small proportion was being seized by the excise men, the amount of goods that were being smuggled during this period is anyone's guess! For example, the revenue service estimated that five thousand barrels of brandy were landed on the Gower coast within a period of six months in 1795.

The smugglers' objective of course was to make money, but there was also an element of nationalism involved in Wales, Scotland and Ireland, where the tax was seen as an 'English tax'. For example, Lewis Morris, who worked for the revenue on Anglesey in the eighteenth century, said that people were trying their best to 'beat the English tax'.

With Napoleon's defeat in 1815, peace came to these shores, and less tax was required to fund the military. Over the next few decades the call increased to establish Free Trade which involved abolishing tolls to help international commerce. As part of this campaign, Sir Robert Peel abolished the duty on some 1,200 items between 1842 and 1845, 450 of these in 1845 alone, and reduced the tax rate on a number of other commodities. This substantial reduction in its profits undermined the illegal trade.

According to the Commissioner of Taxes:

> with the lowering of taxes, and the abolishing of all unnecessary constraints, there is much less smuggling and a great change in the sentiment of the public relating to it. The smuggler no longer has general sympathy, as a romantic hero; and people are starting to awake to the mistake that his offence not only cheats the country, but also steals from the legal merchant. Smuggling is now confined nearly to tobacco, spirits and watches.

However, to make up for the tax lost on these goods, Sir Robert Peel, in 1842, raised income tax by seven pence in the pound!

Since Britain was no longer at war with its continental neighbours, there was less need for ships to guard its shores. The English Navy was by now better organised and as the Empire was involved in fewer military conflicts throughout the world, many of its men found employment with the coastguard service which had been established in 1829. The revenue service now had more ships and men available to them. Cottages were built along the coast to house coastguards who would keep watch for any suspicious vessels, and a mounted force was formed to give chase to the smugglers. In this way they were no longer having to rely on local militias, who had never been particularly enthusiastic in performing these duties. With these measures in place, smuggling became less profitable and gradually declined so that by 1860 there was very little of it going on.

In 1860, the Trade Agreement with France was responsible for the abolition of most of the remaining taxes leaving only a modest tax on tobacco and spirits. In 1864, the Commissioner of Taxes reported, for the first time ever, that no smuggling runs had been reported during the previous year. Smuggling by then was the work of the occasional individual hiding tobacco or a bottle of spirits in his bags as he entered the country. The reason for smuggling had now ceased to exist and the traditional smuggler had finally been defeated.

The Watch House, New Quay

The Smugglers

In the eighteenth century Dr Samuel Johnson's describes a smuggler as 'a wretch, who, in defiance of the laws, imports or exports goods without payment of the customs'. However, smugglers, or 'free marketeers' as they were sometimes called, enjoyed widespread support, at all levels of society.

Certainly there were some evil and cruel men in their ranks. On the other hand, the government by raising exorbitant taxes, had given a free rein to such men, who were then able to depend on the support of the common people as well as the gentry in perpetrating their illegal activities.

Many of the smugglers were fishermen and sailors who sailed small merchant vessels along the Welsh coast. As experienced mariners, they knew all the hidden bays and creeks along their particular stretch of the coast, and their occupation gave them an excuse to be out at sea.

The scale of the smuggling varied from individuals who wanted to avoid paying tax on some goods in order to make a few pence profit, to large international companies with representatives in several ports. Some of these companies were huge, owning large warehouses where goods imported from the far corners of the globe were kept before being smuggled to other countries. They often had influence with those in high places in government and commerce in those countries which were recipients of their contraband.

There was, also, a very sophisticated network for receiving and distributing the goods. The scale and methods are comparable to those of the Mafia in America during prohibition in the 1920s when beer and spirits from Canada, Mexico and the Caribean islands were smuggled into the U.S. and sold in illegal drinking and gambling dens.

Such was the scale of smuggling in Britain during its golden age between the 1690s and the 1850s, that the government lost huge amounts of income. It is estimated that in 1729, for example, the British government lost at least a quarter of the income that it could have earned from taxes on imports.

'The Smugglers', George Moreland

The smuggling firms

Large smuggling firms worked mainly out of Brittany, France and the Channel Islands, utilising the Isle of Man, until 1765, and Ireland, until 1800, as staging-posts for bringing their goods closer to the shores of western Britain. Amongst the larger firms were Andrew Galway and Co. (with centres at Nantes, Dublin and Liverpool), Wors & White Co., Duer Park & Co. and Copinger & Co. They would buy goods legitimately on a large scale from international trading companies such as the East India Company. It was the process of transporting and landing the goods in Britain that was illegal, as they were deliberately avoiding paying taxes on them.

These large companies had organised networks of smugglers working for them throughout Britain. Ships would carry the illegal goods to the shores of Wales, where they would be met and off-loaded by an efficient system of landers and distributors who would take the materials on to the end of their journey. Investors would provide funds for smugglers to buy goods overseas, sometimes giving them as much as £500 – a large amount of money in those days – to go to France in order to purchase brandy and similar goods.

Naturally, in times of war between Britain and France, there would be a ban on the import of 'enemy' goods, but there was still a ready market for French wines and brandy. At such times the French government would be more than willing to help the smugglers in order to undermine the British economy and to take advantage of this propaganda opportunity as part of the psychological warfare waged between the two countries. By smuggling spies into Britain with their contraband cargoes, smugglers could also help France's war effort in another way.

Everyone participating in smuggling activities had his own particular job to do, each one with its own title:

The runners

It was the runners who carried the illegal goods on board ships to the Welsh coast. Many of them were Irish, smuggling salt as well as commodities from France to Wales. Amongst the most prominent of these runners were the brothers John and Michael Connor who operated in the 1770s with their two ships, the Bridget and the Mary Catherine, sailing to Wales and north-west England from Port Rush and Dublin, together with another individual called Connah, operating out of the Isle of Man and supplying the north coast of Anglesey, y Gogarth (*Great Orme*), Morfa Rhuddlan and Deeside. There were also many Manxmen amongst the runners, playing an important part in supplying the northern coasts of Wales and Bae Ceredigion (*Cardigan Bay*).

Welshmen were also involved, of course. Men such as John Garret and the Jean from Deeside, John Messery and the Le Tris from Swansea. At Barmouth there was Maurice Griffiths with the Liberty, John Jones and the Catherine, Rhys Edwards and the Unity and, the most well-known of them all, Thomas Jones and the Dispatch. In Llŷn, the Cefnamwlch family had a small armed vessel which landed illegal goods on the islands of Tudwal and Enlli (*Bardsey*), while in Abergele Ellis Jones landed his contraband in the creeks and channels of Morfa Rhuddlan. In south Wales, two of the most famous runners were Thomas Knight who owned many armed vessels, operating from his base on Barry Island and, at a later date, William Arthur, who, for a time, was the head of a large gang of smugglers at Penarth and Barry.

The smugglers' ships

In the early years of the eighteenth century the runners used small ships, many of them completely open, without a deck, to smuggle goods from Ireland and the Isle of Man. These ships were lighter and easier to handle than the usual trading vessels when landing contraband on rocky shores or in treacherous estuaries. For example, the Mary Catherine was only 16 tons, under the command of the Irishman, John Connor or 'Jack the Batchelor', one of the most notorious and dangerous smugglers supplying the shores of Wales at that time.

Also, smugglers came to favour ships with fore and aft rigging which made the vessel much easier to handle in tight spaces. A larger crew was also required to operate these lively little craft and to unload cargo rapidly. Previously, ships with square rigging had been more popular, but such vessels could only visit narrow creeks when the wind was favourable and they would have to wait for the wind to change direction before they could escape out to sea. But with smaller fore and aft sails, the runners could sail into any creek, unload the cargo and then go back to sea before the revenue men arrived. The smugglers' ships also had large sails so that they could sail at speed when necessary.

The runners favoured ships with a shallow draught, so that they could get much nearer the coast than the cutters which had a deeper draught. The revenue men usually favoured the cutter as it could carry more arms. It was also of a more solid construction and could thus ram the smugglers' ships when they were trying to board them without causing damage to themselves.

Smugglers' vessels were also cheap to build thereby minimising the loss if they were caught. The usual cargo would be some 80 barrels of spirits.

When smuggling became a problem at the beginning of the eighteenth century, the government banned ships under 15 tons whether or not they were operating legally, as they were so often used by smugglers. However the smugglers started using larger ships, so the restriction was raised to 30 tons, and by 1721 ships of up to 40 tons had been banned.

To begin with the revenue vessels were faster and many smugglers were caught as they tried to escape, but some ships, especially the Irish wherry (a small open ship or boat with sails), had oars so that they could row out of the reach of the revenue men when there was no wind. The smugglers could also row into the wind – something the revenue ships could not do as they were totally dependent on sails. Some of the wherries had been built especially for smuggling with more pointed bows than was usual so that they could move faster through the water. They were described as 'slight and sharp' and 'remarkable fast sailers' by Captain William Gambold, master of the revenue cutter Pelham of Beaumaris. In 1779, an act was passed prohibiting anyone from using a boat or ship with more than four oars on board.

However, it was not only ships built specially for smuggling that were used. There is a record of the ferries from Holyhead to Ireland being employed for smuggling purposes. In July 1771, for example, the ferry Jenny was apprehended with rum and brandy on board. Ships carrying cheese and guns from Chester would smuggle brandy to London which had reached Chester illegally from the Isle of Man. Also ships carrying coal from Mostyn, such as the Speedwell, often carried contraband. In June 1757, the Success of Caernarfon, carrying coal from Whitehaven, was caught with 56 pounds of tea and 14 gallons of brandy. The captain of the revenue cutter was invited by Thomas Wilson, the master of the Success, to his cabin for a drink and was offered a fistful of gold if he turned a blind eye to the smuggling. He refused!

Up until 1765, smugglers favoured small ships as they could bring goods right up to the shore, but when in that year, the Isle of Man was lost as a base for smuggling they had to use larger vessels as the goods had to be carried from Brittany or France. These larger vessels were much better armed and much more willing to fight against the revenue cutters. Between 1772 and 1780, there are descriptions, of large armed ships (up to 200 tons) unloading tea and spirits unhindered along the coast of north Wales. One revenue officer reported that one such vessel 'cruised arrogantly along the Merionethshire, Caernarfonshire and Anglesey coasts for 3 weeks and no Officer dare go near'.

When the American War of Independence broke out in 1776 and later the war with Napoleon (1793-1815), merchant ships were given permission to arm themselves against the enemy's privateers (private warships). Naturally, many of the smugglers took advantage of this. In 1773, for example, the Fox, a ship of 100 tons with a crew of 45, was being used to smuggle goods along the Bristol Channel, Cardigan Bay and off the coast of Anglesey. The revenue cutter, the *Hector*, spotted her near Bardsey and sailed to Milford Haven where she enlisted the help of two other cutters, the Lord Neath and the Cardigan. The three ships pursued the Fox in Cardigan Bay but the smugglers were too fast for them and their ship escaped. According to records the Fox was landing about £20,000 worth of contraband along the coasts of Wales every year.

When a ship was seized by the revenue, her owners would apply for her release alleging that it was a member of the crew who had brought the illegal goods on board without permission. Usually this ploy would be successful. Similarly, if any horses had been seized carrying smuggled goods, the farmer would claim that they had been stolen by the smugglers and they would be returned to him!

In November 1768, the *Racecourse*, sailing between Caernarfon and Aberdysyni, had to seek shelter in Pwllheli harbour and the customs officer found unlicensed tobacco and snuff on board. The ship was seized but following an appeal by Richard Evans, a tobacco merchant from Caernarfon, she was released. His argument was that he had bought the goods in Liverpool during July and August and that there was a licence for them, but that the captain had forgotten to take it with him. Evans was believed and the ship released.

If a ship was not released, then the revenue officers would sell her at auction. Usually, however, the buyer would be someone acting on behalf of the smugglers or the original owner. According to the customs officer at Beaumaris there was one ship which had been caught three times and repurchased on each occasion by its original owner. To stop this practice, it became customary for the revenue officers to saw any smugglers' vessel they seized into three parts before breaking her up into smaller pieces and selling them as firewood.

1. An Atlantic wherry, ideal for bringing goods close inshore; 2. A revenue cutter off Ramsgate, fast and heavily armed; 3. Beaumaris, site of the customs house and base for a revenue cutter.

The landers

Waiting on shore for the smugglers' ships were the landers. The function of the landers would be to arrange for the goods to be received from the ships, to carry them ashore and to hide them prior to distribution either to a main agent – a local merchant or to a number of local receivers. The landers would arrange horses, carts and men to move the goods. Usually, half the men were needed to unload whilst the rest, often armed, would keep a watch for the revenue men.

The landers were usually fishermen or men working on the shore, and in some areas they would be assisted by miners, farmers with their horses and carts, and anyone else who was so inclined. People would also help by hiding the contraband in safe places or by giving the smugglers information on the movements of the revenue men or by acting as spies. They would, of course, be well rewarded for their efforts.

Landing goods was the most dangerous part of the opperation. To guide the ships, a special lamp was sometimes used by those on shore to signal that the coast was clear – a lamp with a narrow spout so that its light would only be seen by the ship out at sea. In Talacre Hall, Flintshire, there is a cave at the entrance to which stands the effigy of a bull. Behind the bull's head is a firing box which it is believed would be ignited to tell smugglers out at sea that it was safe to land.

When the revenue men were in the area it was important to warn the smugglers both ashore and at sea. In the Bridgend area, a bell would be rung if a smuggler was caught, so *'that the whole town may rise to rescue the prisoners'*. Bonfires would also be lit as a warning for the ship not to come ashore, but once the revenue men understood their significance it became illegal to light a bonfire near the shore. Another way of warning was to place a white blanket on the roof of a cottage.

It was hard work carrying the contraband up the rocky shores in the dark. The method used to carry four gallon barrels, or ankers, was to tie them in pairs, one on the chest and the other on the back with ropes passing over the shoulders and allowing the arms to be free for balance. This was a method used by Ifan Rewig

Aberogwr, near Bridgend

when taking spirits from Porth Ceiriad in Llŷn up the cliff path to Cilan.

A pair of ankers would weigh over a hundred pounds or fifty kilos. It is hardly surprising that the landers would try to avoid fighting with the revenue men, and would often leave the goods on the shore and flee.

If the goods needed to be transported over a long distance, horses would be used, with each horse carrying between three and four casks. The smugglers would inform the farmer that they needed his horse or horses on a particular night, and he would usually be more than happy to assist them and to keep quiet. Naturally, he would receive a cask of spirits, salt or a packet of tea for his pains. If he refused to help, he might find his implements smashed, his horses injured or his barn set alight!

If his horses were caught being used by the smugglers, the farmer would say that they had been taken without his knowledge, and they would be returned to him. Sometimes horses really were taken without their owners' permission, such as those of Ann Owen of Penrhos, Anglesey, who complained in a letter to her brother in May 1738 that her servant Owen Williams was overworking the horses as he would '. . . *take ye Horsis yt carried ye Corn to the Mill in the day time to cary Run goods in the night time*'.

One of the biggest problems that farmers in coastal areas faced was attracting workers. A few nights helping smugglers paid much better than a week's work on the farm. A farm worker would receive about eight shillings a week but could earn more than ten shillings a night helping smugglers. Being out at night several times a week meant it was very difficult getting up in the morning! According to a member of parliament from Suffolk at the time: 'For all the young clever fellows of the county are employed by smugglers . . . they find a much easier and more profitable employment than any they can have from the farmer, and while they are thus employed all improvements of land must remain in suspense.' Thomas Pennant in his *Tours in Wales* (1778) writes that agriculture had improved greatly on Anglesey after smuggling from the Isle of Man had ceased, '. . . before that time every farmer was mounted on some high promontory, expecting the vessel with illicit trade . . . '

1. *Porth Dinllaen, Llŷn; 2. Llangrannog, Ceredigion; 3. Abercastell, Pembroke.*

Tunnels

There are many stories of landers in Wales using tunnels to carry goods from the shore to safe hiding places. At Llanunwas manor, near Solva in Pembrokeshire for example, it is said that there is a tunnel from Ogof Tybaco (*tobacco cave*) in Aberllong to the home of the Laugharne family, which had a reputation for smuggling and for wrecking ships.

The Old Swan Inn near Barry was also a centre for smugglers, and there are stories that a tunnel ran from the inn to the shore. Behind the inn there are secret stairs which at one time led to the attic, and to this day one of the rooms is much smaller than it should be owing to the hidden stairs in the wall.

It is also said that a tunnel ran from Hen Borth on the eastern shore of Anglesey to Mynachdy farm. At one time this was the home of a Dr Lloyd, who fostered a young boy who had been rescued by a smuggler called Dannie Luckie from a boat off the Skerries as he was about to rendezvous with a ship bring in an illicit cargo. This young boy, who was named Evan Thomas, was the first of the famous family that became known as the Anglesey Bonesetters.

Some say that a tunnel runs from Y Gegin Fawr in Aberdaron to the beach and another from the building on the opposite corner (which is now a cafe and shop) and passes under the cemetery to the beach. Again in Llŷn, a tunnel is supposed to lead from the beach under Tyddyn Isaf farm near Tudweiliog, which explains why the sound of waves are sometimes audible in the farmhouse. Another tunnel ran from Llety Honest Man Inn near Mostyn to the beach which was used by local smugglers.

Stories of smuggling tunnels are common right around the Welsh coast and some are being re-discovered even today. When David Edwards's basment store room flooded in his Ocean Blue shop at New Quay in 2016, he discovered an old tunnel leading to the sea shore below.

1. Ocean Blue, New Quay;
2. Gegin Fawr, Aberdaron;
3. The Old Point House, West Angle Bay.

Carriers and distributors

Once the illegal goods had been brought ashore to secret hiding places, they would have to be transported, sometimes over long distances, to various customers.

In 1799, a group of thirteen men had collected a cargo of untaxed spirits in the Penrhyndeudraeth area and were transporting the casks by horse and cart from the river Dwyryd, over Bwlch Carreg y Frân towards Dyffryn Clwyd. One of them, a weaver called William Jones, was caught and brought before Denbigh magistrates. The Judge asked him, 'What did you sell in Maes y Mynan?'

'The same thing, sir, that you bought off me a week ago,' replied William Jones and was duly released! After gaining his freedom, it is said that the weaver went home to Berllan Helyg to fetch more illegal goods which he kept in a secret cellar under his bed!

In a letter dated June 1784 there is a reference to smuggled goods being carried by mules from the estuary of the Artro in Meirionnydd all the way to Shropshire!

A smuggler named Jolly used to land goods on the beach at Tan-y-bwlch near Aberystwyth from where they would be transported overland by the Welsh drovers to England. A fight took place between Jolly and revenue officers near Llanafan and he and his men had to flee through Pontrhydygroes, leaving dead and dying comrades.

While some smugglers would transport their goods openly through village streets under armed escort, others were less conspicuous. In 1820, Boaz Pritchard, a merchant from Caernarfon, delivered brandy to his customers in a hearse! There are also references to 'pregnant' women carrying spirits in 'belly canteens', bottles holding two gallons, under their clothes. At Trearddur, Anglesey, Ogof Beti was named after a large lady who used to carry spirits in this manner.

On one occasion a cart full of casks travelling along the narrow lanes of Llŷn was stopped by customs men. When asked what was in the casks, the driver replied that it was water from a holy well, Ffynnon

1. Tan y Bwlch cove; 2. Ffynnon Gybi.

Gybi, on its way to the local priest and he was able to continue on his journey. In fact, the casks contained spirits that had recently been landed at Porth Dinllaen!

Silvan Evans in *Ystên Sioned* (1882) refers to distributors of smuggled goods in Ceredigion. A certain Enoc y Brandi ' . . . undertook the role of public auctioneer in remote areas without having paid so much as a farthing for a licence. His modus operandi with the brandy and other spirits would be to place them in baskets on the back of his horse and cover then with salt herrings.'

Aber-cerrig-gwynion near Llandrillo-yn-Rhos

Armed escorts

To guard the carriers as they journeyed inland from the beaches with their spoils, required armed men. They carried either a cutlass, knife or long club, sometimes up to five feet in length and often with a piece of iron on its tip. These clubs were very effective against the revenue men's swords and could easily knock a man off his horse. Many of the guards also carried guns, and many battles were fought between the two sides. Superiority in numbers often meant the smugglers would get the better of the revenue men or that they would be left well alone. David Thomas, in his book on Caernarfonshire's maritime heritage, describes the difficulties facing officers from Conwy at Llandrillo in 1761 when a large crowd of some two or three hundred were unloading goods on the beach. The officers were pelted with a hail of stones, despite their firing at the crowd.

Smugglers ships, particularly the larger vessels, would be ready to assist the landers by providing them with an armed escort. 'No Officer dared approach them, for they always sent armed men to deliver goods in safety,' reported the Beaumaris Customs Officer with regard to the Fox which landed off the coast of Anglesey in August 1773.

Ten years later in 1783, the Beaumaris officer reported regarding ships from Ireland: 'The Crews escort them to any part of the Country well armed and daringly bidding defiance to the King's Officers when they endeavour to arrest them.'

Sometimes frightening people, either by threats or other means, was enough. At Aberdaron, on the tip of Llŷn, a story is told concerning the ghost of Pendre. Often, during the night, lights could be seen going from Pendre down the hill and through the village to the beach and back. According to some this was the ghost of Pendre, but more probably it would have been men transporting illegal goods from the beach. Certainly talk of a ghost would be sufficient to keep some people well away and if anyone asked about the lights, the ghost story would have provided a convenient explanation.

The support of the local community

The landers depended on the total co-operation of the local community. Farmers and their workers along the coast would help to land the goods, supplying horses and carts for transportation to a safe store. They would be rewarded with a cask of spirits or other goods, not only for the help but also for keeping their mouths shut. The smugglers would also bribe people to turn a blind eye to what was happening in the area. One smuggler from Caernarfon is said to have paid £400 annually to keep people quiet.

The smugglers could depend on the support of the majority of the local populace, and in some areas along the coast, there were hiding places in most houses to conceal the goods until it was safe for them to be moved on. In some towns, it is said that every merchant was either a smuggler or was dealing in smuggled goods, that every tavern was selling drink that had been smuggled, and that contraband was being bought by every gentleman and magistrate. Even the church was helping the smugglers. Not only were the clergy buying their brandy, but the goods were sometimes hidden in church buildings and cemeteries, especially in chest tombs.

When John Wesley preached in 1743 in Cornwall against smuggling, referring to it as 'a detestable practice', he was pelted with eggs and stones. Wesley would even refuse to drink tea as it would more than likely have been smuggled! In Wales, the Methodists were also fervently against smuggling, as was the Church – officially at least. The Bishop of St Davids would order the annual preaching of a sermon in all churches in the Diocese against smuggling and wrecking. However the clergy were more than happy to avail themselves of brandy and other goods sold at 'reasonable' price. In June 1774, revenue men found a box containing 86 pounds of smuggled soap in the house of Huw Gruffydd, Tŷ Mawr, Edern on the Llŷn peninsula. Mr Gruffydd was one of the pioneers of Methodism in the area!

1. Caernarfon quay under the castle;
2. St David's, Pembrokeshire.

Throughout Wales the smugglers received support from the gentry, not least in Anglesey. On 12 December 1738 William Bulkeley of Bryndanu, Llanfechell, records his attitude to smuggling laws in his diary: 'I set out . . . to hear . . . informations against persons offending against the cruel and terrible Act against smuggling . . . the proofs against them not being fully and clearly shown (considering the terribleness of the statute and the penalties annexed to it) we acquitted all three.' On 2 July 1739 he records how he: 'Met in the evening the Collector of the Customs of Holyhead at Hugh Price's House to hear an information against the smugglers. Condemned the goods seized, but discharged the persons complain'd of from any penalties.' Not only was William Bulkeley prepared to acquit smugglers but, from time to time, he would also buy illegal goods from them. The entry in his diary for 21 September 1742 reads: 'Paid a Flintshire smuggler that was come to Cemaes from the Isle of Man, 25/- [£1.25] for 5 galls. of French Brandy, which I think is right good!' In other entries, he also notes that he has bought gallons of rum, claret and white wine.

Bulkeley was not the only gentleman on the island to get his hands on untaxed alcohol. Fourteen of Amlwch's leading citizens went for a holiday to the Isle of Man in a 25 ton sloop belonging to some of the most prominent men of the county, including a doctor and a customs official. When they returned, they were accused of smuggling alcohol and the sloop was impounded. They appealed to senior officers in the customs service, claiming in their defence that they had bought the drinks legitimately to be drunk on the way back. Unfortunately bad weather had prevented them from opening the hatches. Their story was believed and the sloop was returned to them. If they were telling the truth, they must have had quite a party in mind, as on board the sloop were seven dozen bottles of wine and four gallons of rum, to be shared between 14 people, including the local parson!

In some areas, smugglers had a secret sign to show which houses were 'safe' and where there were friends to help them. One sign was the bottom of a glass bottle cemented into the wall under the eaves.

1. Custom House, Holyhead (far left in this engraving); 2. Cemaes a haven for smuggling from the Isle of Man; 3. Douglas Inn at Cemaes.

Hopefully, the revenue men would remain unaware of the significance of such signs!

Ordinary people were also very keen to get their hands on these commodities and in some cases if they did not have the money to pay for them, they would barter with farm produce. Brynffanigl Uchaf near Betws-yn-Rhos in Denbighshire, was one such place where agricultural produce would be exchanged for salt and spirits and other smuggled goods. The contraband would be brought in from Llanddulas and there was an arrangement whereby a look out would be kept from the highest windows in the farmhouse for flashing lights indicating that the goods had arrived on the beach.

On Felin Fraenan beach near the bend in the main road between Llwyngwril and Llangelynnin in south Meirionnydd, smugglers would land salt. According to tradition, the women and children of the area would walk miles to the beach taking goods such as butter and eggs with them to a place called Carreg Halen (*salt rock*) where they would barter them for smuggled salt.

On the northern coast of the Llŷn peninsula, on a slope above the village of Trefor, there is a ruin called Uwch Foty. Its local name however is Tŷ Halen (*salt house*) as it was here that the locals went to buy untaxed salt.

Because their ships were slower, the smugglers were always afraid of being caught by the revenue cutter with a cargo of illegal goods. Many ships had hidden compartments in their cabins and hull for the concealment of illegal goods.

Some would hide illegal items among legitimate goods; for example, tobacco would be hidden in casks of legal cider. Some smugglers had special bags under their clothes to hide tea or lace. In some cases crew members would carry up to 30 pounds of tea under their garments and the term 'bootlegger' came from the practice of smuggling tobacco ashore hidden in their boots.

When the *Windsor* of Aberystwyth, carrying lime from Red Wharf Bay in Anglesey, in August 1764, was being searched, one of the officers noticed that there were a large number pots of butter on board and that they were much lighter than they should be. He dug his fingers into the butter, and found that bags of tea had been put into the pots with a layer of butter on top to hide them!

Often, rather than bringing the ship ashore where she was more likely to be caught, the goods would be unloaded into boats and carried to the shore.

Another trick, when being pursued by the revenue cutter, was to rope the casks together and tie them to a large stone and then throw the whole lot overboard unobserved on the side of the ship furthest from the cutter. Later, the landers would go back with a boat to retrieve the casks by hooking the rope and dragging them ashore. This method was frequently used by ships passing along the coast whereby casks would be sunk at a convenient shallow spot. Local fishermen going to retrieve their lobster pots would later surreptitiously bring ashore more than just their pots.

The smugglers of Flintshire had a special type of boat for smuggling salt from Cheshire. There was a hatch in the side of the boat and if the revenue men were after them they would open the hatch and let the seawater wash the salt out of the boat! It is said that Huw Andro of Llŷn had a similar craft.

And even after the contraband had been seized, some smugglers did not give up. In September 1786, David Roberts of Borth y gest near Porthmadog appeared in court, accused of preventing the customs officer and his assistant from doing their work on Traeth Bach. According to the evidence, the customs officer had seized an illegal cargo of salt but Roberts, at Trwyn y Penrhyn, had seized it back, and ' . . . rescuing out of the possession of the said Andrew Paynter [the customs officer] a boat and ten bags of prohibited salt after seizure.'

The proceeds from smuggling were so substantial that It is said that smugglers could make a profit if they were only able to land just one cargo in every three. This would usually be sufficient to make up for the loss of an occasional ship.

Fighting and military assistance

As the illegal trade grew, more and more people took part, until on occasion there were gangs of several hundred men involved in some localities. Sometimes, the smugglers were daring enough to land the goods in broad daylight and there were numerous battles with the revenue men and, from time to time, with soldiers. Fatalities occured on both sides.

The work of the revenue men could be very dangerous. In a report published by the revenue service in 1736, it was said that 250 revenue men had been attacked or injured since Christmas 1723, and that six had been killed.

Pembrokeshire was among one of the most dangerous places to be a revenue man. Lord Cawdor of Stackpole Court was determined to catch the smugglers operating in the area, and in November 1801, on hearing that there was a suspicious ship anchored in Freshwater East Bay; he rushed to the scene accompanied by the local customs official. When they arrived they saw a large number of casks on the beach with boats ferrying more from the ship. Cawdor and the customs official tried to seize the casks which were on the beach and to arrest the landers. But the landers attacked them, and Cawdor was badly beaten. Only one smuggler was caught and he was taken to a house in Trewent, but his companions attacked the house and released him!

Smugglers were not the only danger faced by the revenue men. It is recorded that Lewis Williams, a tidesman from Holyhead, ' . . . as he was going out of the Custom House on his duty, was met by a Boar, which bit him on his knee, and hurt him in such a manner that he was disabled from Duty.' When Williams returned to his duties, he fell as he mounted his horse and hurt the same knee!

When the revenue service felt that they did not have the resources to deal with the smugglers, they could call on the help of the military. This happened in Pwllheli in 1796 when eighteen smugglers landed in the town, behaving exactly as they pleased until a company of mounted soldiers

Freshwater East Bay, Pembrokeshire

drove them back to their ships.

Generally speaking, professional soldiers and their officers could usually be relied on to do their duty, but some of the local voluntary militias were not so reliable and often would have strong smuggling sympathies. But even the soldiers were not always keen to risk life and limb to help the revenue men as they were often outnumbered by well armed smugglers. Also, as pay in the army was poor, many of the lower ranking officers were ready to be bribed to keep well away from any illegal landings. A few revenue men, although they were paid reasonably well – between £30 and £40 per year occasionally took bribes. A lander could make up to £3,000 from a large run and thus could well afford to offer a bribe to make life easier for himself.

There are instances of militias actively supporting the smugglers. There is an example of this in 1806 at Llan-non in Ceredigion, when fierce fighting took place between revenue men and local people. It is interesting to note that many of those who attacked the revenue men were members of the local volunteer militia. Their commander was Mr Strike, allegedly 'the greatest smuggler in Wales'

at the time.

On another occasion in Pembrokeshire in 1825, the Pembrokeshire Sea Fencibles found a hidden store of illegal rum and vodka. To avoid having to write a report about the find, the officer in charge simply ordered: "Drink the evidence men!".

A group of Welsh Fusiliers on duty in Suffolk on 1 December 1747 were somewhat better organised. A unit under the command of Lieutenant Dunn had been ordered to assist customs officers in preventing a smugglers' cutter from leaving goods in a bay near Sizewell. However, the smugglers were so numerous that the soldiers had to retreat – to a nearby pub! The soldiers remained there for half an hour until a band of thirty armed smugglers on horseback arrived in the courtyard. When Lieutenant Dunn saw them he ordered his men to drink up and to get outside at the double. He called on the smugglers to surrender but the smugglers fired at them. When the troops fired back the smugglers fled and two of them were caught.

Aberporth on the Ceredigion coast

Punishment and dangers

Smuggling was viewed by the authorities as a serious offence, and the fines were very heavy. The punishment for injuring or killing a revenue man was hanging and the body would then be placed in a gibbet as a public warning to others. This involved tarring the corpse, wrapping it in chains and putting in an iron cage which would be suspended from a strong wooden frame, and left in a public place for a length of time.

It was not only the revenue who would prevent the smugglers from bringing goods on shore. The sea itself also was fraught with dangers. Two smugglers' vessels got into difficulties off the coast of Anglesey in 1763. The *Molly* was carrying rum, sugar and cotton from Monserrat in the Caribbean to the Isle of Man when she was wrecked in Holyhead Bay. The *Phillipe* also suffered a similar fate when she was driven onto the rocks in the north of the island.

The Isle of Man

Until the beginning of the fifteenth century, several regions of the island of Britain, seaports in particular, were excempt from of taxes, but gradually the ports came under the jurisdiction of the English monarch. Sir John Stanley had been gifted the Isle of Man by Henry IV in 1405 and it remained as 'private' property until 1765 when the English crown reasserted its right to the island. Until that time, Manx ports were free of taxes and it was from here that a great deal of illegal goods were smuggled to Wales and north-west England during the seventeenth and eighteenth centuries. The Isle of Man was a poor place and dependent on fishing until a businessman from Liverpool came to the town of Douglas at the beginning of the eighteenth century to exploit the fact that the island was fiscally independent of England.

The island rapidly became a very important centre for smugglers and large ships laden with multifarious goods would come from Jersey and Brittany (Nantes and Lorient were the main centres) and even from north America to the Isle of Man. Here their cargoes would be kept in large warehouses from whence they would be distributed by smugglers along the coast of Wales, Scotland and the north of England in smaller vessels of less then 50 tons. These were far more suitable for bringing the cargoes right to the shore in the dead of night. In April 1763 Captain Gambold of the revenue service at Beaumaris described the methods of the Manx smugglers who would hire ships known as Irish Wherries, weighing some 30 to 50 tons with a crew of 10 and which would: 'come ashore at midnight, took an hour to unload. Local farmers carted the load . . . bonfire lit to warn if trouble [i.e. to call for help]'.

It is said that during that period every Manxman was a smuggler and all the Crown was able to do was to station officers in the main ports, but they had no rights to do anything other than watch. They could not raise so much as a pennyworth of tax. If the officers wanted to send a message to warn the mainland that goods were on their way, the

Coastal map of Dulas, Anglesey, chartered by Lewis Morris in 1748

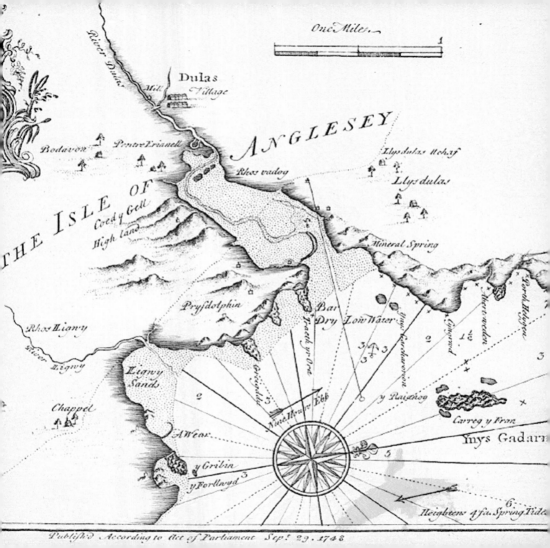

One Mile.

River Dulas

Mill

Dulas
Village

ANGLESEY

Bodavon   Pentre Erianell

Rhos vadog

Llys dulas Uchaf

Llys dulas

THE ISLE OF

Coed y Gell

High land

Mineral Spring

Prysdolphin

Bar
Dry Low Water

Rhos Lligwy

River Lligwy

Lligwy
Sands

3   3
3

2

Ynos Caerhaveien

Gingroid

Pool Helygen

Harn medin

2

3

Chappel

A Weir

y Gribin

y Forllwyd   3

Nine Ways Ebb

Grisially

y Ratshos

Carreg y Fran

5

Ynys Gadarn

3

6

Heightens 4 fa. Spring Tide.

Publish'd According to Act of Parliament Sepr. 29. 1748

smugglers would be there and gone long before it arrived.

The ships smuggling from the Isle of Man to north Wales included a number of Welshmen among their crews. According to the diary of William Bulkeley, Brynddu, on the 29 June 1739:

> Last night the Custom house Cruiser took off Cemaes bay a Large boat comeing from the Isle of Man with Brandy etc. and carryed them to Beaumares. 3 of the crew were of this neighbourhood. Owen Edwards of this parish a very poor man and father of 5 small children, Rowland Morgan and John Prich'd Samuel a Shoemaker of the same parish.

However, not everyone from the island was happy with its smuggling. In 1742 the Bishop of Man wrote:

> Our people are mightily intent upon enlarging the haroubrs at Peel, Ramsay and Douglas; but the iniquitous trade carried on, on the injury and damage of the Crown, will hinder the blessing of God from falling upon us.

A dramatic change came about in 1765 when the Isle of Man was reacquired by the British government and £70,000 compensation paid to its owner Lord Atholl. A bargain indeed, bearing in mind that the Treasury was losing up to £750,000 a year from missing excise duties as a result of smuggling from the island!

When the revenue service was established on the island shortly after that, the officers had to be very careful as to how they dealt with the Manxmen or else they were likely to have had a rebellion on their hands. Apart from the excise levied on new goods reaching the island, nothing, therefore, was done to prevent smuggling the contraband which was already in store to the mainland.

This ploy worked and within a short space of time there was much less smuggling taking place than previously. According to the Excise Collector at Beaumaris in 1766: 'not a twentieth part what used to be in the same period . . . as soon as their old stock of Spirits and Tea are disposed of there'll be no more Smuggling from the Isle of Man.'

The authorities now faced the problem of trying to persuade the Manxmen to follow a lawful career such as fishing and so no taxes were levied on salt on the island to enable them to salt their catch. The Manxmen soon discovered that there was more profit to be made from smuggling that salt back to mainland Britain than from fishing!

Because of the loss of the Isle of Man as a convenient centre for the distribution of goods, the runners now had to reorganise themselves. From now on goods had to be transported all the way from Brittany, France or the Channel Islands which meant using much larger and faster ships. These were much better armed and since both the ship and its cargo were more valuable, the smugglers had more to lose. Consequently they were more aggressive and more prepared to fight against the authorities.

In May 1767 there is a report of a smugglers' ship from France which had come to re-establish business in north Wales following the loss of the Isle of Man. It had unloaded most of its cargo in south Wales before sailing to Anglesey and then to Morfa Rhuddlan. At Morfa Rhuddlan, some twenty armed men came ashore to guard the unloading and to provide an armed escort for the carts. They left 6 blunderbusses, 6 muskets, 7 pistols, 13 cutlasses, a carriage gun, a swivel gun and one hundred pounds of gunpowder for future use.

In 1770, John Connor attacked the revenue ship Pelham Cutter which was under the command of Captain Gambold, sinking it near Beaumaris. Between 1772 and 1780, an armed smugglers' ship (of some 200 tons) was brazenly unloading tea and spirits along the northern coast. In 1775. A big Irish cutter (150 tons) with 30 crew came to land goods in northern Anglesey, the Great Orme and Morfa Rhuddlan. It stayed for a fortnight, having first parked itself in the Strait opposite Beaumaris and threatened to blow up the coastguard's house if any steps were taken against her. She was left well alone!

Ireland

Having lost the Isle of Man as a convenient distribution centre, Port Rush near Dublin, came to take its place to a large extent. There is evidence that smugglers in the Dee estuary who previously had been dependent on the Isle of Man played a prominent role in this development.

The inhabitants of north and west Wales acquired many of their duty free commodities from Ireland, which was not part of Britain until the Act of Union of 1800. This meant that Ireland was excempt from duties up to that date. In Dublin and at other ports, there were huge warehouses for storing goods from France and other places. Smugglers would later distribute these goods to Wales and the north of England.

In Wales there was a great demand for salt to preserve meat, butter and herrings, but the salt was very heavily taxed. Through much of the eighteenth century it would cost as much as four pence a pound, but in Ireland it cost only a penny a pound. This generated a lucrative market for the smugglers, who would buy their salt in Ireland for a penny a pound and sell it in Wales for two pence a pound. At twice the retail price this was a fine profit and still only amounted to half the taxed price.

The authorities were aware of the problem and a survey was undertaken in 1740 with members of the Salt Board going from port to port, but often noting that 'smuggling does not occur here' which begs the question whether the inspectors were either accepting a backhander or else that the inhabitants knew they were on their way and had managed to hide the salt.

Because of its close proximity to Ireland, Wales was an important destination for contraband goods from Port Rush. Ships from Ireland however would not always take the quickest route, tending to avoid many of the western coasts, particularly when the weather was unfavourable, as the seas were shallow and ships could easily go aground when the wind was from the west. For this reason, they often sailed towards the southern coasts which were safer for bringing their goods to shore.

Offshore islands off the western coast were ideally placed for smuggling from Ireland – such as the islands of St Tudwal, Llŷn

It would frequently be Breton or French crews who would convey goods directly to Wales and they would welcome a short break in some sheltered waters off the Irish coast, where there was little chance of their being caught, while they waited for an improvement in the weather and the right tide to make the passage to unload their cargo on the coasts of Wales.

At the end of the eighteenth century, a man called Morgan O'Connell was in control of smuggling operations on the west coast of Ireland. His son, Daniel O'Connell, would later become a prominent figure in the struggle for Irish independence.

All along the coast, teams of men would wait for ships from Ireland to bring tea and spirits to the shore. In Milford Haven and Swansea, this sometimes took place in broad daylight and if the customs officers tried to stop them, the smugglers would be sure to put up a fight. There was no respect for the revenue ships either. In 1770, three ships carrying twenty four smugglers from Ireland came across the revenue cutter Pelham at anchor. The Pelham was boarded and the revenue men were lucky to escape with their lives. The cutter was later found wrecked and stripped of everything on the rocks of Ynys Dewi (*Ramsey island*).

Aber-llong (llong: *ship*) *near Solva, Pembrokeshire – a westward facing haven*

Place-names near Cei Newydd referring to where salt (halen) *was landed*

The Revenue Men

The revenue service was initially established in the thirteenth century, when taxes were first imposed on certain goods. Over the years, the service was extended, and customs houses were built in ports as bases for the collector and other officials and where confiscated goods were stored.

By the eighteenth century, with smuggling rife, and the government losing substantial sums of money as a result, a service was established to police the coasts and to catch the smugglers. These were the revenue men or excise men. Their routine duties were as follows:

'They came on duty at dusk and went to bed at dawn. Every night they were assembled in the watchroom, armed with pistol and cutlass or with musket and bayonet . . . no man was given his instructions until he reported for duty and he was forbidden to communicate with his family after he received them . . . the guard was inspected twice a night to see if it was alert and watchful.'

In 1800, the revenue service had 40 ships carrying a total of 200 cannon, together with their crews comprising some 700 men. On each ship there was a captain, a mate and a crew of sailors depending on the size of the vessel. They were expected to be out at sea, especially at night and during bad weather as these were the times that smugglers usually operated. However, with so much money being made through smuggling, it was tempting for the revenue men to turn a blind eye to what was happening in exchange for either a financial bribe or a cask of brandy.

*The Lady Mary Leighton –
a revenue ship, 1830-40*

They did, however, receive a fair wage and could supplement it with rewards paid for results – that is, any untaxed goods they seized would be sold and the proceeds shared between the revenue men and the ship's owner, after the government had received its half share (the 'King's Share'). Most of the ships used by the revenue were privately owned, hired by the Customs Board, their owners receiving a share of the value of any illegal goods seized.

The revenue officers wore red shirts and blue trousers, while the officers, the captain and the mate, wore a long blue coat with brass buttons, the button holes being embroidered with silver thread, and a cocked hat and cockade. Each officer was armed with a cutlass and pistol.

Every revenue vessel had a narrow pennant which was flown from the mast. However, this flag was only allowed to be shown when they were bearing down on the smugglers and there was a rule which stipulated they could not apprehend a ship suspected of smuggling without first raising the flag. In some cases, smugglers' ships would fly a similar flag to confuse the revenue men.

As well as having men on ships and in the customs houses, the service had officers patrolling the coast on horseback – the riding officers. These were established in 1698 and were stationed along the coast, up to ten miles apart depending on the terrain and how much smuggling took place in the area. The chief riding officer would be responsible for six officers and would ride back and forth along the coast checking on his men and keeping an eye on the beaches and coves for any evidence of smuggling. If one of them saw or heard of suspicious activity, he would gallop to fetch the rest of the riding officers in the area to form a posse to try to apprehend the smugglers. Also, if a suspicious ship was sighted out at sea, the marine revenue men would be informed so that they could board her. However, the authorities were concerned at times that some of the riding officers were being bribed to keep their eyes and mouths shut. According to Sir William Musgrave, Commissioner of Taxes:

'They never ride out except on their own private business and they fabricate their journals. Some of them are agents and collectors for the smugglers and they are not resolute enough to prove any serious obstacle to large bodies of armed smugglers.'

The revenue services also had officers in the ports – the landwaiters – who would inspect foreign goods being unloaded; coastwaiters who would inspect goods being transported from other British ports and tidewaiters, who would either be tidesurveyors who had a boat to visit each ship as they reached port, or tidesmen who were placed on each ship to supervise the unloading. Not all these officials were efficient in their work. Lewis Morris described coastwaiters in mid-eighteenth century Anglesey as: 'Two Fools, one Rogue, one Bully and one Numbskull.'

But to be fair, the work was not always easy. According to one report, Foulk Jones, a coastwaiter at Amlwch, and two tidesmen went out to a large cutter 'in the King's Boat . . . & were ordered to keep off or they wo'd fire upon them'.

Not everyone could become a revenue man and there were restrictions on what they could do. They could not invite their wives or their friends on board ships, nor could they accept a gift or favour from a captain or mate, and any candle used below decks had to be in a lantern. This was because a smuggler could extinguish a candle and then either overpower the revenue man or quickly hide any contraband. Anyone joining the service had to swear an oath of allegiance before a magistrate. Lewis and William Morris, in one of their letters, mention visiting the Quarter Sessions at Beaumaris to swear an oath of allegiance to the king and receiving certificates to prove it, signed by two magistrates. Tidewaiters could not operate as merchants, brokers or owners of public houses, neither could they attend political meetings. Also, two responsible persons had to act as character witnesses before they could be offered a job with the revenue service.

To prevent revenue officers from becoming too friendly with the local inhabitants, few local people were appointed to these posts, and they would be moved from one area to another fairly frequently so as not to put down too many roots. In 1826 it was recorded that most of the revenue men at New Quay, Ceredigion, were from the south of England. The only

Welshman amongst them came from Tenby and there were some who came from as far away Ireland. Naturally, this did not go down well with the locals, and the fact that very few of them spoke or even understood Welsh put them at a serious disadvantage when it came to carrying out their duties efficiently.

But whatever their backgrounds and however restrictive their conditions of service, the authorities would never be totally reliant on the integrity of these officers. In 1744, Robert Wynne of Bodysgallen near Llandudno wrote a letter to the squire of Boduan, who was the member of parliament for the boroughs, asking for his assistance in appointing

Bodysgallen, near Llandudno

someone suitable for the post of tidesnan for the Conwy customs house, instead of someone whom he described as a 'pimp' for Mrs Holland Conway. 'I need not tell you how serviceable it will be to me to have a ready, willing fellow upon the King's boat upon this troublesome river.'

One revenue man who was not entirely honest was Owen Owens, who started working around the rivers Glaslyn and Dwyryd in Meirionnydd in 1745. He was in the area for eighteen years and failed to catch hardly any smugglers! At last, the authorities put pressure on him to do something and very soon afterwards, in 1763, he seized the Speedwell, an 18 ton open boat from Deeside which was smuggling gin and brandy from the Isle of Man. But the captain complained that Owens had been in cahoots with the smugglers all the time! As a result, Owens lost his job and was jailed for two years.

But being bribed by smugglers was not the only problem for the revenue service. As much of the illegal goods consisted of alcohol, this was a temptation in its own right for some, in particular Robert Thomas, a revenue man from Anglesey, who was drunk after 'piercing a puncheon of rum on board the Perky from Antigua'. On another occasion he was 'intoxicated with Liquor' on the Lovely Match and 'Commonly Disguis'd in Liquor and very incapable to take care of the Trust reposed in him'!

However, in all fairness, the revenue men were always short of manpower and resources, and it was too easy for the smugglers to get the better of them. An example of the odds they faced comes from Newhaven, Sussex, where in June 1733, the revenue men tried to seize ten horses carrying tea, but as they were accompanied by thirty armed smugglers, they had no chance and were taken prisoner until the illegal goods had been transported from the area.

There was a similar incident at Arundel, again in Sussex, in July 1735. The smugglers knew that the revenue men were watching them, but they were determined that they were going to land their goods. They therefore kidnapped the officers and held them captive until the goods had been brought ashore.

A similar incident occurred in Pwllheli in September 1791. When customs officials boarded a ship in the harbour to inspect its cargo, they were incarcerated in the cabin for five hours – sufficient time for the crew to unload the tobacco and gin which was on board. By the time the revenue men were released, the buyers and their carts were long gone.

1. Beaumaris Court;
2. Entrance to Pwllheli harbour.

Paying for information

Another method of trying to catch the smugglers was by paying for information. A parliamentary act allowed the revenue service to pay up to £50 for information that would lead to seizing untaxed goods and to the capture of at least two of the smugglers and their conviction in a court of law. There was £500 available for information which would lead to a conviction for injuring or killing a revenue man. But fearing revenge against themselves or their family, informers were few and far between, although there are some examples. One was the seizing of four chests containing over 300 pounds of tea from the attic of Dr G Frances Lloyd, a gentleman who later became sheriff of Anglesey. He had paid a guinea for the tea but was caught after someone told the revenue men and the informer was given 'one guinea for each chest with a promise his name would not be mentioned.'

This was not the only case of its kind. A smuggler called John Jones was given a lesser jail sentence after he gave information to the revenue service. After writing a long, grovelling letter to the authorities saying that he was starving in prison and that his wife and children were reduced to begging in order to obtain a little bread for him, he was released early from Caernarfon Gaol on condition that he served on the revenue cutter, the *Pelham*.

Coastal maps of possible smugglers coves around Milford Haven and Cardigan, drawn up by Lewis Morris

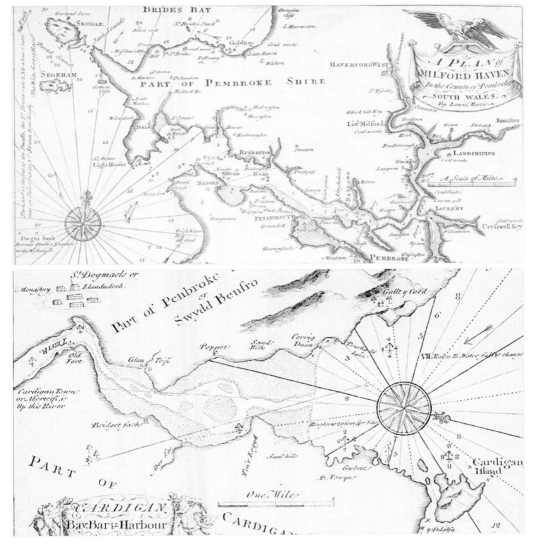

Smuggling and the law

In 1745, an act was passed allowing the owner of any ship caught loitering within five miles of the coast or in a navigable estuary to be brought before a magistrates court, and, if unable to provide a good enough reason for being there, he could be sentenced to a month's hard labour. From 1746 onwards, anyone injuring or killing a revenue man would be sentenced to death, and anyone found guilty of smuggling would have a choice between paying a fine, going to prison or joining the navy.

Local authorities could also be fined. A county could be fined £200 if illegal goods were discovered within its boundaries. If a revenue man was attacked in the county, the county authorities would have to pay a fine of £40, and if an officer was killed, the fine was £100. However if the smuggler responsible was caught within six months the fine would be revoked.

It was not only smugglers who appeared before the courts. There are several cases of revenue men being brought before the court on charges of killing or injuring smugglers in the performance of their duties! According to one member of parliament during a debate in the House of Commons in 1736:

> In some parts of the coastal counties all the people take part in smuggling making it impossible to appoint a jury which will, in a court case, do justice to the revenue officer . . . these inquests always find the officer and his assistants guilty of murder . . . although it is evident that they were defending themselves.

There was an instance of such a case in Caernarfon in July 1783 when a small sloop which was used for smuggling along the Menai Strait was captured. In the ensuing fight, one smuggler was killed and a revenue man injured. The smugglers were kept in Caernarfon gaol overnight, but such was the sympathy and support for them in the town that the magistrates released them the following morning! The smugglers brought a case of murder against the revenue service, but were unsuccessful.

1. The Anglesey inn at the entrance of Caernarfon port was the revenue office at one time; 2. It was later moved to this building near Porth yr Aur.

There were also other restrictions on the revenue men whilst carrying out their duties. If they seized a ship and were unable to find any illegal goods on board, the owner could claim compensation – although, most probably, the goods had been thrown overboard before the revenue cutter could come alongside. To pursue a ship without being certain of its illegal intent would not help to further an officer's career. Also, the revenue cutter could not stop a ship outside territorial waters without good cause. Otherwise they could be accused of piracy, which was a defence used by many a smuggler.

Therefore, the revenue cutter skippers had to be sure of their exact position when seizing a ship. Here is part of the instructions to revenue ship captains issued in 1832:

> When a ship is seized, the officer should take special care to immediately note the depth as well as the distance from land to two points on the shore at the exact time the ship was seized and that in the presence of two or more officers . . .

Compensation

Up until 1808, there was no compensation for officers injured or killed in the line of duty. From that year onwards, a pension of £10 per annum was paid to any member of the customs service who lost an arm or a leg. The Crown would also pay for any surgery needed, and the widows and orphans of any officer killed would also receive a pension.

Before this development, sustaining an injury could be catastrophic. Whilst boarding a ship in the south of England, one revenue officer grabbed a rail to haul himself onboard, but one of the smugglers brought his cutlass down on the officer's two hands, cutting the fingers off so that he fell backwards into the sea. In the days before any pension, it would have been very difficult for that man to make a living for himself and his family after such an incident. Luckily, a petition was brought before Parliament granting that officer a pension and creating a precedent for compensation to other officers in the future.

At one time, permission was given to private ships to pursue smugglers and if they succeeded in capturing them they could keep any goods seized. But they would have to convince the Commissioner of Customs that they had only seized the goods of proven smugglers and not those of innocent traders carrying out legitimate business – otherwise they would be no better than pirates! In fact, some smugglers took advantage of this situation in order to attack their competitors!

In 1822, the use of privateers to apprehend smugglers came to an end and the present day Coastguard Service was established. The officers of this new service were a combination of ex-naval men, former members of the cavalry who had been employed as riding officers, as well as some who had no previous military experience.

Improvements were also made to the organisation and methods of the revenue ships at this time. Rather than staying on board their ships during the hours of darkness, either at sea or in port, their crews would now patrol the shores,

1. *Custom House, Cardigan;*
2. *Government offices at the quayside, Pembroke Dock.*

rowing in small boats to the various beaches and creeks. There were also coastguards on the cliff tops looking out for suspicious vessels – each officer with his musket, spyglass and a one-legged donkey stool (if an officer fell asleep on such a stool he would fall over and wake up!). The officers also received much better pay, as well as a reward of £20 for each smuggler caught.

William Gambold

One of the most daring and successful revenue men was Captain William Gambold and his ship the Pelham Cutter which guarded the coasts of Anglesey and north-eastern Wales. Such was the smugglers' fear of him, that the Collector of Customs at Beaumaris reported that '. . . several of the present set of smugglers have declared that if they meet with the Pelham Cutter, they will sink her, and threaten the Land Officers very much.' The revenue service's answer was to provide Captain Gambold with a larger vessel which would be as fast as the smugglers' ships. Gambold normally worked out of Beaumaris and his usual method of catching smugglers was to send one of the two boats carried by the Pelham with '10 or 11 hands and surprise them in the night when they are going to land their cargo'. This worked well in catching the smaller ships, but he often complained to the authorities that he did not have the resources to do his work effectively against larger vessels.

At other times, he would rely on the speed of the Pelham to pursue smugglers in daylight. For example, in May 1765 when he spotted a ship with its sails furled within two leagues of the Skerries off the north Anglesey coast he decided to pursue her. The smugglers raised their sails and headed for the Isle of Man, but after a chase that lasted three hours the Pelham managed to capture them. On board the revenue men found 30 casks of brandy, two casks of wine, 846 pounds of tea, 224 pounds of liquorice and 40 pounds of tobacco.

Naturally, receiving information about the movements of the Pelham was of great interest to smugglers, especially concerning those rare occasions when she was in dry dock being repaired. At those times, the smugglers were busier than usual, and Gambold would change his tactics. 'During the time the Cutter was under Repairs we sent both her Boats along the coast, with the Commander in one and the Mate in the other.'

Gambold and his crew would receive a share of the value of any cargo seized; ten shillings a ton, for example, for the cargo of the William & Mary which was running brandy from the Isle of Man in 1765. Sometimes there would be disagreement between revenue cutters working in the

same area. In 1763 Captain Robertson of the Lord Howe asked for a decision from the Beaumaris Commissioners with regard to Gambold's crew's right to a share of the profit from goods seized from a ship when it was the crew of the Lord Howe who had boarded it.

At other times, co-operation was essential. For example, when a well-known smuggling ship was sighted sailing between Anglesey and the Great Orme, the Pelham, under Gambold's command, and the Hornet, under the command of Sergeant Cross, followed her. The weather deteriorated, however, and the smugglers escaped. When the Hornet returned to Beaumaris and the Pelham to Holyhead, news arrived that the smugglers had already delivered their contraband to an agent in Amlwch.

The Morris Brothers of Anglesey

Probably the most famous Welsh customs officials were Lewis and William Morris from Anglesey. They were enthusiastic letter writers and made a considerable contribution to the Welsh literature and scholarship of their day.

Lewis Morris (1701-65) was appointed as a customs officer in Holyhead and Beaumaris in July 1729, a post which he held until 1743 when he was followed by his brother-in-law, Owen Davies. Lewis' colleagues included a deputy collector, a landwaiter, a tidewaiter and four tidesmen.

His brother Richard composed the following *englyn* [a Welsh verse in strict metre] to him around the year 1731:

To Officer Lewis Morris,
for apprehending the Smugglers' Soap

> Lewys, mindful man, is it true –
> That you seized the goods of the poor?
> The soap thief is a haughty type
> Hiding in deepest Anglesey.

Lewis Morris answered that the tax was 'a just one ...to support our countries'.

In 1736, it is recorded that he seized 49 gallons of brandy which was being imported illegally on the Anne & Deborah. Between 1737 and 1744, Lewis was commissioned to make detailed charts of the coast between Pen y Gogarth and Milford Haven. Such charts were needed to avoid shipwrecks but also to help the revenue ships to become familiar with every creek and beach along the coast in their attempts to stop smuggling.

His brother, William Morris, was appointed Deputy Overseer of Customs at Holyhead in March 1737, and often he would sign his letters to his brothers, 'Eich caredigawl frawd, Gwilym Gontrowliwr' [Your sincere brother, William the Controller]. He received a wage of £20 per annum but could increase it substantially with fees claimed on goods seized. He described his work as 'a grey cat watching hundreds of mouse holes all at the same time'. In one letter he notes that the inspector received 'yesterday . . . £21 more

1. Lewis Morris; 2. The Lewis brothers' memorial near Dulas, Anglesey.

than me for one seizure of silk handkerchiefs . . . and there are goods secure in the customs house . . . which will fetch [£]30 or 40 more I hope . . . ' In October 1760 he mentions in a letter to his brother Lewis: 'I must go to the Customs House to measure the seizures to be placed in Gambold's cruiser to be taken to Beaumaris and from there the goods from India will be taken to London.'

He also refers to selling goods which had been seized and to a Captain Morgan who had 'large boxes full of tea which he seized a while ago and which he had bought in the Customs House.' He knew well that the gentry of the island dealt with the smugglers, and, according to a letter to his brother Richard, they had become a 'den of runners, the gentry turned smugglers'.

What chance did the revenue service have of catching the smugglers? In reality,

not much, because it is said that those trying to stop the smuggling were outnumbered ten to one by those involved – not to mention the many thousands that took advantage of the illegal trade. With such general opposition to paying taxes on imports, it was extremely difficult for the revenue men to do their duties. They received very little support from the general public and details of their movements were sure to reach the smugglers and their helpers on land.

Neither was there much incentive for the revenue men to risk their lives trying to catch those involved. A rare example, therefore, is the incident in 1795, when the revenue man George Beynon and a detachment of soldiers succeeded in attacking smugglers on Rhosili beach and overpowering them. The smugglers fled leaving behind a hundred casks of good wine.

Certainly, there are cases of revenue officers making a name for themselves, and substantial amounts of money by way of their share of the seized goods, and there was many a cutter captain who wanted to make his mark with an eye on getting a better job in the navy later on.

But the priority of many of them was a long, uneventful career – doing what was needed, and no more. Many of the revenue officers were learned and cultured men and it is not surprising that some of them came to prominence in other fields rather than their everyday work. One of these was the Scottish poet Robert Burns, who was a customs officer in southern Scotland, whilst in Wales we had Lewis and William Morris as well as other members of this famous literary family. One wonders would Burns and the Morris brothers have been as productive and well-known today if they had spent their time and concentrated more wholeheartedly on their careers with the revenue service?

Rhossili beach, Gower

Smuggling along the coastline

The pattern of smuggling in north and south Wales was very different. Whilst smuggled goods arrived in north Wales from Ireland and the Isle of Man, it was from the Channel Islands and France and even further afield that south Wales received most of its contraband. South Wales had one great advantage; its proximity to Bristol, the main British port for trade with the New World with a substantial population eager for duty-free goods. It was easy enough for a larger vessel to transfer at least some of its cargo to smaller boats whilst sailing up the Bristol Channel and then to report its loss overboard in a storm at sea. Customs officials could often be bribed, not only in Bristol but in the smaller Welsh ports as well.

French ships would also transfer some of their cargoes to smaller ships in the Bristol Channel, especially onto vessels carrying coal and lime from south Wales to south-west England. In 1718, the Swansea Collector of Taxes sent a letter to the Customs Board stating that he had seen 'between Clovelly Roads and the island of Lundy two French ships laden with wine and brandy and other goods' and that 'A great clandestine trade is carried out on in that Channel between the smuggling vessels and the vessels employed in carrying limestone from that part of Wales into Devonshire'.

A survey was conducted in 1681-2 of the ports of western Britain, from Poole in Dorset to Swansea. It was found that smugglers did not have to bring their goods ashore in isolated coves and beaches as the customs officers in the ports were not carrying out their duties. According to the report, they were all very much like the Swansea customs boatswain: 'a cunning old man who does nothing for his wages; he has a boat but no oars, and he admitted, when he had oars that he would never go out to the bay.'

Many of the illegal goods came from the Channel Islands, and at least one smuggler from Guernsey, Richard Robinson, sailed his ships regularly to the

Bristol Channel islands off the southern coast of Wales: 1. Lundy; 2. Flat Holm; 3. Steep Holm.

Glamorgan coast during the 1730s. He himself was captain on the largest of these vessels, while another was under the command of his son, Pasco. They would initially bring illegal goods to Flat Holm, and then, when it was convenient, to the coasts of Glamorgan and Gwent. Illegal goods from the Continent would also be unloaded on the islands of Lundy, Caldey, Skomer and Skokholm before being transferred later to the south Wales coast.

Lundy

In November 1781 a gentleman called Peter Fosse reported to the Customs Board:

> We think it is our duty to inform you that we have received intelligence from undoubted authority, that large quantities of tea and brandy are frequently discharged out of armed smugglers from France and lodged on the island of Lundy till opportunities offer for putting the same on board pilot boats belonging to this port [Ilfracombe], and land the said goods on the coasts of Cornwall, Devon, Somerset and Wales.

Lundy, in the Bristol Channel, was an important centre for smuggling. According to the Cardiff collector of taxes in the eighteenth century, 'Never there lived yet a man on the island of Lundy who was not connected with smuggling'. Lundy was described as being 'encircled with inaccessible rocks, so that it cannot be assaulted . . . so precipitous . . . that one man well armed may repel and keep down many . . . ' Large ships would call there from France and the Channel Islands, leaving goods which would later be transferred to smaller ships for transportation to the coasts of south Wales and the west of England.

Lundy began to be used for smuggling following John Score's purchase of a lease on the island in 1721. Only on one occasion during Score's time on the island, were revenue men successful in seizing goods. It was very difficult to surprise the smugglers as the revenue men could be sighted a long way off and after they had landed, they would find themselves faced by the huge cliffs which protected most of the island.

Smuggling ceased for a while after Score left in 1729, but restarted in 1743 when Thomas Benson turned the island into a fortress for smuggling. Benson had a fleet of a dozen ships trading with America and the Mediterranean, bringing tobacco and wines to the island. The goods were initially landed in the ports of the west of England, but then Benson would insist that they were not intended for the British market but rather for re-export to other countries, and thus no taxes would have to be paid on them.

Benson was a very influential figure, a successful merchant, the Sheriff of Devon, and later on the member of parliament for Barnstable. He used his contacts to win a contract to transport prisoners to Virginia and Maryland at £20 a head. However, America was not to be their destination. Instead they would be brought to Lundy where they were used as cheap labour to turn caves into warehouses (one of these still exists on the island and is known as Benson's Cave), and to pack tobacco into handy little packages to be smuggled to south Wales and the west of England. But although Benson made a great deal of money, he was in debt, including £8,229 in unpaid taxes to the Crown for that part of his business which was legitimate. Much of this money had gone on paying bribes to those in high places.

Benson had an idea, however. In 1751 he announced that he was taking a cargo of tobacco from a warehouse in Dunstable to Morlaix in Brittany. His ship, the Vine, left the port for Milford Haven. Here, the captain declared that he was going to France but six days later he was in Briton Ferry, not far away – with an empty ship. The Vine could never have sailed to Brittany and back in such a short time.

The revenue men strongly suspected that the tobacco had been left on Lundy and four officers from Barnstable went to the island. In the meantime, however, Benson, having very likely been informed that the revenue were on their way, made sure that his own men and tobacco were nowhere to be found when the officers arrived. There was plenty of other evidence, however, to show what had been going on! A number of ships were later seized with illegal tobacco on board which could well have come from Lundy. Benson failed to clear his debts, even after an unsuccessful insurance claim on a ship which he had deliberately sunk. He subsequently fled to Portugal.

In 1785 the island became a refuge for the Welsh smuggler, Thomas Knight, after he had been driven out of his base on Barry Island. Knight used a wherry to transfer illegal goods from Lundy to the coasts of south Wales and south-west England.

Gwent and Glamorgan

It was not only the islands that were used to land illegal goods. There was many an estuary which was also suitable for this purpose. With their strong tides and currents, local knowledge was essential to navigate them safely. The estuaries of the Usk, Rhymney, Taff and Ely were convenient for landing illegal goods as there were plenty of small channels which could be used to hoodwink the revenue men.

Aberthaw was also popular with smugglers, because if the revenue men tried to catch them on one side of the river Dawan it was easy enough to row across to the other! A lack of boats meant it was impossible for the revenue men to catch their quarry, as one of the officers complained to his superiors in London:

At Aberthaw and Barry when any boat goes out to em from thence, the Owners of em have always a Spye on the officer; and when they find him on one side of the River of Aberthaw, they'll land what they have on the other; and by reason there's no Boat in the Service, not any boat on those acco'ts to be had for love or money, and the Officer obliged to go to a bridge about two Miles round, they have time enough to secure the goods before he can get there . . . there is instances that they have run'd goods in the day time before the officers face in this Manner. At Barry tis the same; if they find the officer on the Iseland, and the officers can't get over till the Tide is out, wich may be five or six hours . . .

The officer added that there were plenty of places to hide the goods on the island. In fact, the revenue officers had little chance of catching smugglers in this area as their resources and manpower were so scarce. Two officers were drowned whilst returning from the islands of Flat Holm and Steepholm where they had been searching for illegal goods, and in 1773 officers refused to go to Flat Holm in bad weather because their boats were in such poor condition.

A merchant by the name of Thomas Spencer erected a fortified building

1. *The Blue Anchor inn, Aberthaw;*
2. *Nash Point, Glamorgan.*

around Marsh House at Aberthaw, in which to store tobacco and other illegal goods. They would remain there until the market prices were at their highest when he would sell them to obtain the maximum profit. In 1750, there was so much smuggling in the area that the authorities asked for the assistance of an armed ship to deal with the smugglers who were operating between Sully and Aberthaw, Barry Island being their headquarters.

When Thomas Knight's infamous band of smugglers established themselves on the island in the 1780s, things became even more difficult for the authorities. Knight had a fleet of smuggling ships and some 60-70 armed men to protect his business. The customs service experienced great difficulties in recruiting officers in this area, so great was the fear of Knight and his men who were only too willing to open fire on revenue men and ships.

In 1772, the Two Sisters was caught landing tobacco and rum on Aberthaw beach. The captain, Edward Michael, tried to bribe one of the revenue men with a jar of rum, but was unsuccessful. In 1790, the Adventure, also from the west of England, was caught landing six casks of rum and ten packs of tobacco in the estuary of the river Ebbw near Newport. The captain and the owner, John Thetone, had hidden the illegal goods in special compartments in the ship's hold.

It is said that smugglers used the river Ogmore to bring illegal goods to Bridgend, and in the words of one revenue man, 'here is a very convenient Bay for small vessels, and I find very great Quantitys of tea is Run here . . . ' It seems it was cobblers who did most of the smuggling in the area. Many of them frequented the New Inn which, at the time, was situated near a bridge over the Ogmore. When the inn was demolished, a cave was discovered under the kitchen which was large enough to hold a full cargo of illegal goods. According to local tradition, the garden of the inn was like a cemetery having being the burial place for so many of the smugglers' adversaries!

The old Custom House, Penarth

Swansea and Gower

Gower was very well known for its smuggling, and for a generation and more this trade on the peninsula was run by the Lucas family of Port Eynon. There were plenty of isolated creeks, caves and beaches on the peninsula, and as Swansea was one of Wales' main ports during this time, it is no surprise that it became one of the most important areas for smuggling. We are reminded of this in the name Brandy Cove given to the beach near Bishopston. Brandy Cove (previously called Hareslade) on the southern coast of Gower was a hotbed of smugglers. From this sheltered bay, transport inland was virtually invisible through the wooded Bishopston valley. Above the valley, farms such at Highway were used as staging posts and William Arthur, Great Highway Farm and John Griffiths of Little Highway were known as daring smugglers in the 18th century. The entrance to an old lead mine by the beach was blown up by customs and excise men to stop smugglers hiding their contraband in the shaft and transporting it to local farms.

Once again, the revenue officers complained that they lacked the resources to tackle the smugglers. According to one report in 1730, 'The smugglers are grown very insolent and obstruct our officers in the execution of their duty . . . the master and the mariners of the ship Galloway . . . came up on deck with pistols and drawn cutlasses and refused them to rummage.'

The captains of the ships carrying coal from Swansea made sure that they were sent by 'strong winds' to Ireland where they would pick up soap and salt, landing their illegal cargoes on the beaches of the Gower.

One method the smugglers had of ensuring that the chief customs officer in Swansea would not hinder them from unloading in the harbour was to make sure that he was called up for jury service in the local court! Of course while he was otherwise employed, it was easier for smugglers to undertake their business. A clear illustration of the support enjoyed by smugglers from those amongst the higher echelons of society, even the judiciary.

Throughout the 1780s and 1790s, there

The Salt House, Port Eynon – there are traditions that there were 'hidden' rooms in this coastal building for smuggled salt

were several instances along the south Wales coast of revenue ships being wrecked and revenue officers injured. The area around Swansea was particularly bad for clashes between the two sides. In January 1788, revenue officers looking for a well known smuggler came across some fifty men armed with 'iron bars, pokers, large knives, whips and other weapons'. In the face of such odds, it was impossible for them to serve a warrant on the smuggler and when they requested military assistance the reply they received from the War Office was: 'the condition of the forces at this time is such that it was not possible to send troops to South Wales' – and this was during peacetime!

But smugglers in the area did not have it all their own way and they had to be very crafty in hiding their contraband. For example, a hiding place was found in the bed of a small river behind the Old Rectory in Rhosili. The only way of accessing it was by changing the course of the river first!

Even if the revenue men succeeded in seizing illegal goods, it was not always an easy task transporting them to the safety of the customs house. In April 1803, a revenue officer called Frankie Bevan seized over 400 four-gallon casks of whisky in Pennard on Gower. They were loaded onto wagons and escorted to Swansea, but during the journey, a 200-strong crowd of drunken men and women began harassing the officers by shouting and throwing things at them. Luckily, the convoy was accompanied by up to fifty members of the local militia to ensure its safety!

1. Brandy Cove, Gower; 2. Entrance to the old lead mine at Brandy Cove; 3. Three Cliffs Bay near Pennard.

Carmarthen and Pembrokeshire

The wide estuaries of the Laugharne, Gwendraeth, Tywi and Taf were very convenient for landing goods, as were the beaches and dunes of Cefn Sidan and Pendine. The coast of Pembrokeshire was full of isolated coves and beaches which were also ideal for smuggling. However, this area was also the location of one of the main ports of Wales – Milford Haven – where the revenue service had its headquarters.

On the whole, owing to the enormous length of coastline to be patrolled and the support they enjoyed from local people, the smugglers faced very little opposition to their operations, although some of the revenue cutters did have the occasional success. For example, in 1788, the *Ferret*, working out of Milford Haven, managed to seize a number of ships in the Bristol Channel. Amongst these was the *Four Brothers* carrying illegal brandy and gin, and the following year it captured the *Success* from Cornwall, carrying 1,085 pounds of tobacco and 280 pounds of snuff, all neatly packed into bladders ready to be sunk to the seabed, to be picked up later by local fishing boats. In February 1789, the Ferret seized the *Polly* from Cardiff carrying nearly 13,000 pounds of tobacco, and two months later, it apprehended the *Morning Star* outward bound from Bristol and carrying 1,557 pounds of tobacco.

Pembrokeshire had the advantage of a long, rocky coastline full of small hidden coves. The southern part of the county, with Caldey Island lying just off the coast, was very convenient for landing goods, as were the islands of Skomer and Skokholm in the west and Ramsey on the northern coast. Ceibwr Bay was a popular spot for smuggling, and in 1807 the local vicar complained about all the brandy that was coming to the area from Cherbourg at a time when Britain and France were at war! In the same year, at Whitesands Bay, the crew of a smuggling ship was arrested by the revenue cutter *Hope*. They were transferring a cargo of spirits to smaller casks. The empty small casks were

The cove of Ceibwr, near Teifi estuary in northern Pembrokeshire

probably hidden and brought to the beach ready to be filled when ships came to the area.

Solva was renowned for its smuggling with caves in the vicinity being used to conceal goods and contraband before being taken to safe houses and hiding places throughout in the area on behalf of the smugglers.

One customs officer, when he understood that the candles used in the local Baptist chapel had been smuggled, marched into the chapel one evening and confiscated them, leaving the congregation in the dark!

1. *Llanunwas manor house, above Solva;*
2. & 3. *There is a tradition that a tunnel connects Llanunwas with the coast.*

Ceredigion

The 'official' taxable trade that went through the Ceredigion ports during the eighteenth century was fairly insignificant – barely sufficient to pay the wages of the local revenue officers. Household goods were imported from Bristol and other places with corn, herring, butter and slates being the main exports. However custom officers' reports of the period note that smuggling was 'rife' in Ceredigion – 'it is practiced daily and is at a very great height all along the Coast, Brandy, Tea, Salt and Sope from the Isle of Man and Ireland and other places are the chief articles . . . and carried mostly in Irish Wherrys'. Certainly, places such as the Teifi estuary, Mwnt beach, Aber-porth, Llangrannog, Cwm Tydu, New Quay, Cei Bach, Aberaeron, Aber-arth, Llan-non and Llanrhystud were well known for smuggling, as were many secluded coves along Ceredigion's long coastline.

Because of the importance of the herring industry, much salt was smuggled into this area. After receiving information from an unknown source in August 1704, John Bevan, a riding officer from Tywyn, and seven of his men had shadowed a number of ships which were unloading illegal salt along the west coast. When they reached New Quay, they came across some a hundred and fifty men with two hundred horses ready to carry the salt from the ships. The eight revenue men had no hope against such a crowd and when the smugglers spotted them, the officers had to fire their guns to defend themselves. This led to the officers being arrested by the local constables, and one of Bevan's men, with the unusual name of Remarke Bunwoith, had to face a court hearing as he had wounded one of the smugglers! It was quite evident that the local magistrate, a Captain Lewis, was sympathetic to the smugglers' cause.

By the 1720s, Aberystwyth was well-known as a centre for illegal goods, but as the local revenue service had not had much success in tackling the smuggling, a special committee of enquiry was established to try to find out the reason why. On one occasion when the revenue officers were brave enough to board a ship which they suspected of smuggling, 'a large gang of smugglers came on board the

1. *The smugglers' cave at Cwm Tydu;*
2. *Penbryn beach; 3. Mwnt.*

ship at night – as many as forty or fifty –
and tied the officers in the ship's cabin,
and then proceeded to unload the goods'.

The Dyfi estuary and Meirionnydd

At one time the Dyfi estuary was a very busy place, full of ships and boats carrying goods such as lime, coal, ores, slates, etc coastwise, and the ports of Aberdyfi and Derwen Las exported cloth produced inland in both Maldwyn and Meirion. But behind this activity, there was another and much more profitable trade – smuggling. Borth beach, the Ynys-las dunes and the maze of river channels on the southern side of the estuary were very convenient for landing and moving illegal goods which were later transported inland.

To the north of the Dysynni estuary there were many suitable coves such as Traeth Felin Fraenan near Rhoslefain, and at Llangelynnin and Llwyngwril. On Felin Fraenan beach is Carreg Halen (*salt rock*). Local people would come to Carreg Halen to buy or barter for salt. There is also Craig yr Halen (*salt rock*) and Ynys yr Halen (*salt island*) to be found in the mouth of the river Mawddach.

It is no coincidence that branches of one of the most famous smuggling routes in Wales – y Ffordd Ddu (*the black road*) – start from Rhoslefain and Llwyngwril,

meandering past Llynnau Cregennen, under the slopes of Cader Idris towards Dolgellau.

Near Y Friog (*Fairbourne*), according to an entry in 1780 in the diary of Elizabeth Baker from Dolgellau, there was a skirmish between the local deputy sheriff, Owen Owens and David Williams of Henddol when he went to collect a £200 debt from Williams for duty payable on goods which had been smuggled. During the siege of Henddol, Owens and two of his bailiffs were shot, although luckily they only suffered superficial wounds.

During the eighteenth century, Barmouth was also a busy port with ships carrying cloth from Dolgellau to every corner of the world. This gave the port's ships a good opportunity to indulge in the illegal trade and to land untaxed goods along the coast before returning to the harbour.

One of the smugglers' main suppliers, Andrew Galway 'Merchant of Nantes,

1. Mawddach estuary at Barmouth;
2. Carreg Halen, Traeth Felin Fraenan;
3. George III Inn at Penmaenpool.

Dublin and Liverpool', had a network of runners throughout Britain, including John Jones of Barmouth and his ship, the *Catherine*, Maurice Griffiths and the *Liberty*, Rhys Edwards and the *Unity* and the most famous of them all, Thomas Jones and the *Dispatch*. Their regular voyages to America and continental Europe were very useful for concealing the fact that they also ran many illegal goods from France, the Isle of Man, Ireland and further afield.

Further up the estuary, the George III Inn was reputed to contain far more in its cellars than those items on which duty had been paid.

The Glaslyn and Dwyryd estuaries

Traeth Mawr and Traeth Bach with their numerous channels and landing places were ideal for smuggling. Ogo Smyglars (*smugglers' cave*) is to be found not far from Aberglaslyn and there is a similarly named cave on Trwyn y Penrhyn above the Dwyryd.

The early 1700s saw the beginning of the quarrying industry at Ffestiniog with slates being brought down from the mountains on horseback and in carts to the banks of the Dwyryd in Dyffryn Maentwrog, before being loaded onto boats to be transported to ships anchored at the mouth of the estuary. The slate boats would return upstream with coal and lime from these ships, often with supplies of tea, sugar, soap, salt and spirits hidden amongst these cargoes. These small craft were more flexible than larger vessels when it came to choosing landing places, and being well informed of the movements and whereabouts of the revenue men, they could make sure that they always landed on the opposite side of the river!

It is said that a relation of the famous Welsh hymnologist, Edward Stephens, (Tanymarian, 1822–1885) would supplement his income as a slate carrier by selling smuggled soap.

Similar exploits took place in the Glaslyn estuary where the smugglers' knowledge of the currents and tides of Traeth Mawr (before the building of the Cob in 1812) was particularly useful. Traeth Mawr was very dangerous because of its quicksand and the landers would always be one step ahead of the revenue men by landing goods and loading their carts in areas where there were dangerous channels and quicksand between them and the officers. Goods were landed from boats that would come up the estuary with the tide, which meant a long journey round before the revenue men could catch up with smugglers, who would, of course, have long since disappeared! On one occasion the revenue men started firing their muskets from across a channel, injuring one of the smugglers. As a result,

1. Traeth Mawr – Glaslyn estuary;
2. Borth-y-gest.

the officers were summoned to appear in court, but the case was dismissed.

It is said that at the beginning of the eighteenth century, a certain Captain Williams lived at Borth-y-gest. After he retired from seafaring, he started dabbling in smuggling, and he was even called Captain Williams the Smuggler! He lived in Plas y Borth and it is said that his house in the evenings was more like a tavern than an ordinary dwelling. *Nosweithiau llawen* (traditional Welsh evenings of entertainment) were held there with copious amounts of beer and wine. The resident harpist would often be the renowned Dafydd y Garreg Wen. It is said that it was on his way home from Plas y Borth that Dafydd fell into a drunken sleep in a ditch, and when he awoke the following morning he heard the lark singing above his head. He was immediately inspired to compose the famous Welsh air, *Codiad yr Ehedydd* (The Rising of the Lark).

Pwllheli and Llŷn

This was a lawless area in the eighteenth century, and smuggling was rife. There were riots in Nefyn in 1724 when an attempt was made to prevent goods from being landed there. These included salt from Ireland which was so essential for the processing of herrings for which the village was renowned.

In February 1763, the *Marie Therese* of Bordeaux brought a cargo of brandy, rum and wine to Porthdinllaen, but as there were not enough revenue men to detain the smugglers, they had to let them go. After unloading her cargo, she sailed to Aberdaron with an Aberystwyth man on board acting as pilot so that she could come ashore safely. The revenue cutter was ordered by the Collector of Taxes to go after her, but by the time the cutter arrived the French ship had unloaded her cargo and was long gone. She was not the only ship by a long chalk to make the journey from France to Llŷn. In Pwllheli, in April 1796, eighteen armed smugglers came ashore from their ship and walked through the town, openly carrying their contraband, whilst the sergeant and his twelve soldiers on duty could do nothing other than observe their passage.

Smugglers would be given a great welcome in Pwllheli, and the commercial success of the town depended to a large extent on illegal goods, such as iron, spices, spirits and salt which were landed secretly on Llŷn's isolated beaches.

The revenue cutter failed to stop smuggling in 1808, after she had sighted a 25 ton ship at anchor in Porth Cadlan near Rhiw. Men were seen unloading sacks from the ship to the beach, but although the cutter went after them they escaped. Later, officers on the mainland discovered two sacks of salt hidden in a potato field on the cliff top.

There are numerous records of coal ships being seized, including the sloop Peggy which docked in Pwllheli in July 1763. A few days after her arrival, the customs officer heard a cart going along the street at midnight. He made enquiries, and subsequently discovered a heap of coal in Thomas Samuel's yard, who admitted that it was the captain of the Peggy who had delivered it from the ship.

Tŷ Coch Inn on the beach at Porth Dinllaen

The Cefnamwlch family near Tudweiliog had a small armed privateer which landed goods on the islands of Tudwal and Enlli (*Bardsey*). She also often sailed to Chester as the family had business connections in parts of Lancashire. A secret tunnel is reputed to lead from Cefnamwlch towards Gwindy, its entrance concealed by a stone in the garden.

During the seventeenth century, Sir William Jones lived at Castellmarch near Abersoch and it is said that he was friendly with a gang of smugglers who used to land goods at Trwyn Llanbedrog nearby. Sir William had a servant he wanted to get rid of. The captain proposed that his men might kidnap the servant, at a price, and take him to the south of France. This was duly carried out, but the servant got on so well with his captors that he became one of them. In time, he became mate of the ship, eventually becoming its captain! Some years later, he decided to return to Abersoch and was determined to play a trick on his old master. Sir William was invited on board the ship to taste the selection of wines that the smugglers had on offer. While he was eating and drinking, the ship left Abersoch and Sir William had to spend some time at sea before his former servant allowed him to buy his freedom and return to Castellmarch.

Rhuol, or 'Porth y Rhiw' as it was once called, is at the western end of Porth Neigwl and is still used as a creek for local fishermen. At one time, it was a small port and ships were built here on a slipway. Rhuol's tavern, Ty'n Borth, must have enjoyed a thriving trade at these times, and was without doubt used extensively for smuggling as well. It is recorded that in June 1824 a schooner on her way from Guernsey to the Clyde called at Rhuol and offloaded lace, tea, brandy and gin. She is said to have stayed there for several days. Richard Edwards the squire at Nanhoron wrote to the customs complaining, that if their cutter had been at St Tudwal's Roads nearby instead of Pwllheli, the smugglers would have been caught. 'Having the cutter at Pwllheli is a waste of time,' he said. 'She might as well be stationed at Charing Cross!'

The old coastal tavern, Ty'n Borth, at Rhuol, Rhiw

Abersoch was also a well known centre for smuggling. According to the captain of the revenue cutter in May 1767:

On the fifth of this month, a sloop of 100 tons anchored late in Aberdaron bay, and ten men came ashore, with swords and pistols, and offered brandy and tea for sale. They said that they came from France, and that they would not sell less than ten casks of brandy and a chest of tea, asking ten pounds each for them. The following evening a gun was fired from the ship to call the men back, and they then sailed to the Cardigan area and sold their cargo there apparently . . .

In letters dated 1783 and 1784, one customs officer states that in a year smugglers had sold £16,000 worth of tea, brandy, wine and gin in the Pwllheli area alone.

Ieuan Dew, the poet, describes Pwllheli at that time:

A heavenly place of joyful drinking
A place attracting all men
They flock here from all quarters
The home of cheap wine and gifts.

In 1814, smugglers were seen unloading salt at Porth Colmon, some of which was found in cottages at Llangwnnadl and Bryncroes. Four men were arrested and as they did not have the money to pay their fines they were thrown into Caernarfon jail. Many appeals were made for their release, especially as their families were now destitute, but all to no avail. The food in the jail was so poor that one of them, William Williams, became thin enough to squeeze between the bars and escape! He eventually reached home where he was hidden in the butter churn. When he was strong enough, he was disguised in women's clothing and left the area, emigrating to the safety of America.

1. *A hidden beach at Llanbedrog;*
2. *Aberdaron; 3. Enlli (Bardsey); 4. Porth Iago.*

Caernarfon and the Menai Strait

With so many ships plying their trade along the Menai Strait and entering and leaving the port of Caernarfon, there were plenty of opportunities to bring illegal goods into the area. But ships had to be careful as they entered the Strait because of the dangers of crossing the bar near Caernarfon to the west and the treacherous nature of Traeth Lafan in the east. The presence of revenue men at Caernarfon and Beaumaris also made things difficult for the smugglers, but there were plenty of places to land and hide goods in the area; around Dinas Dinlle and other beaches on the southern side of the estuary for example, and on Ynys Llanddwyn and the dunes at Newborough on Anglesey from where they would eventually be transported across the Strait in smaller boats at a later date. Bangor, on the eastern end of the Strait, was known as 'a great thoroughfare for smugglers'.

At Trefor and Dinas Dinlle, there were designated salt houses (*Tŷ Halen*) where a supply of smuggled salt could be obtained.

In July 1783, a sloop used for smuggling was pursued and caught in the Strait near Caernarfon. In the ensuing fight, one of the smugglers was killed and one of the revenue men injured. The smugglers were caught and kept overnight in Caernarfon jail before appearing in court the following morning. Although causing injury a revenue man was a serious offence, the smugglers were released, and since one of them had been killed they tried to bring a case against the revenue men, but without success.

In 1806, a smuggling company from Guernsey, *Cartereux Priaux*, had appointed an agent in Caernarfon called Lawrence Banks, who paid £400 a year to bribe officials and to assist smuggling operations in north Wales. At that time, the town's customs house was located in what is now the Anglesey Arms Hotel. The revenue men that worked from here were responsible for patrolling the banks of the Menai Strait and the coast as far as Dinas Dinlle. In 1857, a purpose built customs house was erected in Porth yr Aur from

1. Porth Penrhyn;
2. Menai Strait from Twtil, Caernarfon.

where it is said that smugglers' lights could be seen at night in the dunes at Newborough and Dinas Dinlle.

Caernarfon at the time was busily establishing itself as a port for the export of slate and some captains were even accused of smuggling slates! In 1717, a ship from Caernarfon was prosecuted for carrying more slates than was stated on her licence. This was rather unfair, as it was customary to put extra slates on ships as some were inevitably broken during loading and unloading. However, this would not be understood by the customs officials at every port. It is evident that the loaders at Caernarfon were more careful than those of Porth Penrhyn near Bangor, as six extra slates per hundred were allowed in Porth Penrhyn but only four in Caernarfon. When the loaders were more careful than usual, it was possible for a ship to arrive at port with more slates on board than permitted by her licence. The captain would then be accused of smuggling!

Anglesey

The first collector of taxes at Holyhead was appointed in August 1680, not to stop the smuggling of tobacco and spirits, but to prevent 'great quantities of Irish cattle being imported there in contravention of the Act prohibiting such imports into Britain'.

By the eighteenth century, Holyhead was a small but important port for trade along the coast and was home to a flourishing fishing industry. Irish wherries would bring brandy, rum and tea from the Isle of Man and salt and soap from Ireland to be landed on the Anglesey coast. The island's proximity to the Isle of Man was a great temptation for smugglers, and both landowners and the common people supported this illegal trade.

The northern coast of the island or the Ardal Wyllt (*Wild Country*) was particularly notorious for smuggling. Here there were many impoverished smallholdings and people trying to eke out a living from the land and from fishing. Not far away were the miners of Amlwch who worked in the copper mines of Mynydd Parys. It is said that the miners formed gangs which could be very dangerous to any revenue man. They also had a great thirst for illegal spirits! In the words of one observer :' . . . the Officers are afraid of performing their Duty for the Miners are a set of lawless Banditti . . . '.

In May 1765 there were no less than five ships full of rum from the West Indies in Holyhead harbour. They were on their way to Ireland, but there were only three revenue men to guard them. They sent for assistance from Captain Gambold and his ship the Pelham, but much of the cargo had been unloaded and the ships long gone before Gambold arrived.

According to a report by the Beaumaris Collector of Taxes in 1770, John Connor – or Jack the Bachelor as he was called (Connor was an Irishman and since smuggling was seen as a political/patriotic act in Ireland, Connor was a national hero) – had attacked the Pelham, under the command of Captain Gambold, in Beaumaris bay and sunk her near the town. Captain Gambold was given another ship, the Hector and had some success with his new command; in 1771 he seized

1. Holyhead harbour; 2. Mynydd Parys copper works; 3. Porth Amlwch.

③

the *Speedwell*, a coal carrying ship under the command of Captain Thomas Rowlands, near Bagillt, and also the *Jenny*, a 130 ton ferry from Dublin.

But there were much larger ships than the Jenny along the north Wales coast. The report states that some ships up to 200 tons were unloading tea and spirits along the coast. In 1775, there was a large Irish ship of 150 tons with 12 carriage guns, 16 swivel guns and thirty men on board, running tea, spirits and other goods along the coast. According to a report at the time: 'It cruised arrogantly along the Merionethshire, Caernarvonshire and Anglesey coasts for three weeks, and no officer dare go near.' The ship was in the area for two weeks, and threatened to fire upon and destroy the coastguards house if not left alone. Captain Gambold followed the vessel but kept his distance.

It is said that goods were being unloaded at Beaumaris and that several ships, including the pilot vessel Young Tom, which was described as 'a very remarkable smuggler for some years', had links with inns in the area. For example the Sign of the Coffee in Beaumaris where tea smuggled on the Young Tom was hidden in an outbuilding.

W. D. Owen's famous novel *Madam Wen* was based on some of the smuggling and wrecking traditions of Anglesey.

1. Moelfre beach; 2. A hidden path known as 'The Smugglers' Path'.

Aberconwy, Morfa Rhuddlan and the Dee Estuary

The northern coast was very well-located for smugglers from the Isle of Man. One individual who ran goods from there to Deeside, Morfa Rhuddlan, the Great Orme and northern Anglesey, was the Irish smuggler, Connah. This was the man who gave his name to Connah's Quay, another famous smugglers' haunt. The Old Quay House at Connah's Quay was originally a farmhouse and became an inn owned by Connah following the development of the port from 1777 onwards. The New Cut, a channel along the Dee estuary, had been dug in 1737 making the western shore of Flintshire more suitable for ships than Chester.

One of the most infamous of the Morfa Rhuddlan smugglers was Ellis Jones of Abergele. Before its reclamation from the salt marshes this area was full of creeks and channels, very much suited to the unloading of contraband.

In January 1712, a revenue officer is recorded as having 'lain on his belly in the sun' near Conwy, watching as the entire local populace came with carts and wagons to transport salt. Because of the numbers involved, he was too scared to do anything to prevent them, especially as the leader of the gang was Sir Griffith Williams, a baronet and JP. Unfortunately his hiding place was discovered and he was beaten up, bound and blindfolded to prevent him identifying his captors or discern where the smugglers were taking him. He was taken to Sir Griffith's residence where he was imprisoned in a hen house, and given a little buttermilk. After being released he sent an intelligence report to London, but nothing was done about the incident. According to the official report, the officer was unable to corroborate his story, as everyone involved was either a tenant, a servant or totally dependent on important men in high places.

The Great Orme lighthouse as well as beaches near Llandudno were also used for smuggling and in 1761, two revenue officers, Robert Lloyd and David Jones,

The Great Orme lighthouse

Dyffryn Clwyd as far inland as Corwen and beyond. After 1765, shipbuilding commenced on the salt marshes. According to the Collector of Taxes at Beaumaris, fast ships were constructed there, of a type which had not previously been seen in northern Britain. At a later date, one of these, a 70 ton cutter, was caught smuggling at Whitehaven in north-west England.

In 1765, when the Isle of Man was lost as a convenient centre for small craft to land goods on the coast of north Wales, a change was seen in the supply pattern. Large well-armed vessels now had to come all the way from France. In 1767, such a vessel came to re-establish the illicit trade in the area, and when it landed at Rhuddlan it was accompanied by twenty armed smugglers who offered to 'escort' the carts for several miles inland, and a substantial quantity of weapons and gunpowder were left for the landers to defend themselves in future. They obviously intended the business to be on a permanent basis.

The Dee estuary was also noted for its smugglers as it provided access for supplying the substantial needs of Chester

came across smugglers unloading goods. Out in the bay they saw a wherry from which goods were being transferred to smaller boats to be brought ashore, where a large contingent with horses was ready to transport them. There were not enough officers to stop the smugglers and so they got away scot free, despite chests of tea subsequently being discovered on the beach.

Because of its location, Rhuddlan developed as a convenient centre for the landing and distribution of illegal goods to as well as the gentry of Flintshire. It is said that the smugglers, being more familiar with the dangers of the estuary than the revenue officers, would lure them to perilous coves and into strong currents. One officer who lost his life in this way was Edmonds who was entinced to his doom as he endeavoured to capture the infamous Connah. This story is commemorated in local placenames such as Edmonds's Hollow near Oakenholt.

Thomas Pennant in 1796 talks of a large cargo of wine being landed near Mostyn for the gentry of Flintshire, but that the goods were confiscated by customs officials and taken to the Llety Gonest Inn (Pennant's father was the owner of this establishment). However, during the night, a gang of colliers attacked the inn, imprisoning the customs men and liberated the wine.

One of the officers noticed that the 'colliers' were wearing very fine clothes under their rough miners' garb, as well as gold rings on their fingers! An enquiry was held but 'such was the fidelity of our people that none were captured.' Nevertheless, on another occasion the story ended very differently for a local smuggler, who, according to the Register of Mostyn Paupers, was hanged on the site of the present-day docks.

Spirits and goods were also unloaded in the Dee estuary prior to being despatched to other locations. For example, ships carrying cheese from Cheshire to London would take concealed supplies of brandy to the capital and coal ships and even canal barges taking coal from the pits of Flintshire provided a very convenient means of transporting brandy.

Of all the goods which were smuggled out of the Dee estuary, the most remarkable were ships cannon from John Wilkinson's works at Bersham. These were smuggled to France at the time of the Napoleonic Wars. In the same way, copper sheets for ships' hulls made by Thomas Patten in Holywell were sent to France and the Netherlands again at a time of war between France and England.

> 1. *Llety Gonest* (Hones Man) *Inn, Mostyn;*
> 2. *The Old Quay House at Connah's Quay;*
> 3. *Legend has it that a tunnel, now blocked ran from the shore, under the Coast Road to the cellar of the Old Tavern Inn at Llannerch-y-Môr.*

Some notorious Welsh smugglers

The Lucas Family

Stout Hall, Glamorgan, was the home of this well-known gentry family of smugglers. John Lucas was a handsome man, but had an evil temper and very little regard for the law. He was given Salt House in Port Eynon by his father which he proceeded to fortify and use as a headquarters for his illegal activities, 'storing said stronghold with arms'. He also had another house, Kulverd Hall, which he 'rebuilded and repaired' and '. . . rendered both inaccessible save for passage thereunto through the clift . . .' It is said that he 'secured ye pirates and ye French smugglers and rifled ye wrecked ships and forced mariners to serve him'.

John Lucas went into partnership with two other men from the area, George Eynon and Robert Scurlage, and it was these three who controlled the smuggling gangs that worked along the Gower coast during the eighteenth century.

It is said that Lucas was some sort of Robin Hood character, as the whole of Gower took advantage of the illegal goods that he had brought ashore in Port Eynon. It was quite usual for the smugglers to be generous with the local people in order to ensure their co-operation.

At the far end of Port Eynon is Culver Hole, a cove surrounded by a sixty foot wall with lookout slits. Lucas used it to keep arms and it is said that there was a secret tunnel running to it. During the last years pf his life, he gave up smuggling and removed the fortifications from Salt House. He was followed in the smuggling trade by numerous members of his family.

It is said that a ship belonging to one of his descendants, John Lucas, got into difficulties on Nash Sands, but before he had time to unload his illegal cargo, a band of wrecker and smugglers had emptied her. Lucas rushed off to the house of a local squire who was the leader of this particular group and demanded that his goods be returned. He managed not only to recover his goods but also to find himself a wife – the squire's daughter whom he had never met before!

The Lucas family controlled the area

for nearly 200 years. It is said that seven generations of the same family lived at Salt House and that the last of the Lucas clan died of fright in 1803, as he watched the house being destroyed by a huge storm. According to tradition, the cellars at Salt House were so big that you could drive a horse and cart into them. It was also said that there had been no time to distribute the final cargo of wines and silk from France following the death of the last John Lucas and that they are still in the cellars, but although many people have looked for them over the years, nothing has been found.

One of the family's houses was the Great House at Horton. In 1986, when the owner was undertaking renovation work he found loopholes for muskets in the wall. It is also alleged that the staircase was made of timber from a ship that was wrecked off the Gower coast.

Apparently, the composers Gilbert and Sullivan based their opera The Pirates of Penzance on John Lucas, who not only smuggled goods into Wales, but also along the Cornish coast, near Penzance.

The Culver House, Port Eynon

William Owen

Owen is a smuggler about whose short but adventurous life we know more than any other.

William Owen was born in Nanhyfer (*Nevern*), Pembrokeshire, in January 1717, the son of Owen David Bowen, one of the most prosperous farmers in the parish. Owen received the best education, probably at Cardigan, but he categorically refused his father's offer of sending him to university to prepare him for the priesthood, as well as an offer to be apprenticed as a lawyer. He hated farming and insisted that he wanted to go to sea. In 1731 or 1732, he ran away to Haverfordwest where he joined the crew of a small ship trading with Bristol.

For the next two years he was back and forth between his home and the sea, but during this time he also had to get married (although he later left his wife). His father bought him a small ship but within a year he had lost her when she was seized by revenue officers whilst returning from his first smuggling trip to the Isle of Man!

He then enlisted on a ship that was heading for the West Indies, but after quarrelling with the captain he joined an armed smuggling ship, the *Terrible*. Sometime in 1736, the *Terrible* was pursued by two Spanish coastguard vessels. The captain wanted to flee, but Owen and other crew members wanted to stand their ground and fight. The captain was imprisoned in his cabin while the rest of the crew, under Owen's command, fought a hard battle. Sixty of the Spanish coastguards were killed, 25 of them when Owen rolled a powder keg onto one of the ships, detonating it and creating a huge explosion. Eleven of the crew of the Terrible were also killed, Owen himself receiving a serious wound to his head. They then sailed to Barbados where Owen, in his own words. '[being] a sober and sensible man not given to cursing or swearing, gave himself up to women' who

"The confessions' of a Welsh smuggler" – this unique autobiography records the life of William Owen, the 'hated' smuggler from Cardigan, and other smugglers, and is now kept in the National Library, Aberystwyth. It was written in Carmarthen gaol in 1747 by Owen himself whilst awaiting his execution for murder.

The
Birth, Life, Education
and
Transactions
of
Captn. William Owen
the Noted
Smuggler.

Who was executed for the Murder of
James Lilly at Carmarthen on
Saturday the 2d. Day of May 1747.

Written by his Own hand when under
Confinement, and delivered to Mr.
Daniel James of Carmarthen aforesaid
in the presence of Mr. John Davies the

bore him children 'of all colours'.

He returned to sea but was caught by a Royal Navy ship. The captain thought him 'such a brave fellow' that he offered him a post on board. Owen remained with the ship for twenty months before managing to escape back to Wales.

He resumed his smuggling activities, making a number of smuggling trips from the Isle of Man to the English Lake District and Pembrokeshire. On one occasion he caused substantial damage to one of the revenue's ships off the coast of north-west England, but finally lost his own ship and her cargo to revenue officers, escaping with only a shilling in his pocket. He acquired another ship from the Isle of Man, smuggling goods to Westmorland and Liverpool and, on one voyage, a large consignment of tea to Barmouth.

Then, in April 1744, he was involved in a fight with revenue men who tried to board his ship which was at anchor in the river Teifi. During the fighting Owen and his crew killed four of their assailants, including James Phillips the customs officer and three of his assistants, before escaping back to the Isle of Man. A warrant was issued for his arrest and Owen fled to take refuge in the mountains. He was later caught and taken to Liverpool before being transferred to Hereford for his trial. Owen provided his own defence during the trial and somehow persuaded the judge and jury that he was not guilty and was released!

He went to Ireland, but it was not long before he returned to smuggling, running goods to south Wales. However, this came to an end when his ship was wrecked during a storm in 1746.

He then joined a band of pirates, but caught a fever off the North African coast, and returned to Ireland and from there to Cardigan to recuperate. There he met a friend called James Lilly, another well known smuggler, and it seems that they decided to rob a house in Nanhyfer. During the robbery they shot one of the servants in his face.

The two robbers disappeared but they were seen in Cardigan a few days later, and some local men went after them. Lilly shot the horse of the leader while Owen shot one of the pursuers dead. It is said that Owen then shot Lilly dead in order to take

The Nyfer estuary downriver from Nevern in northern Pembrokeshire

his horse to escape. However he was caught and accused of killing both Lilly and the other man. He was put on trial at Carmarthen in April 1747 and found guilty. He was hanged in May 1747, at the age of thirty, after a short but eventful life.

Siôn Cwilt

He was the most famous of the eighteenth century smugglers in Ceredigion, responsible for distributing illegal goods throughout the area. His story has been popularised in the work of the novelist T. Llew Jones. He lived in a moorland cottage near Synod Inn, an area which is still known to this day as Banc Siôn Cwilt. Some say that the name Cwilt derived from the multi-coloured patchwork coat he wore. He is recorded as John Quilt in the parish records of Llanina when his son was baptised there in 1758, but it is more probable that the name is a corruption of the Welsh word gwyllt, meaning wild, a surname which originates from Radnorshire. He was also known as Siôn Sais ('the Englishman'), as apparently he was not fluent in Welsh.

He was supposed to be related to Sir Herbert Lloyd of Ffynnon Bedr, the county sheriff. It is believed that Siôn came to live in the area because of its central location between Ffynnon Bedr and two well-known smuggling beaches, Cwmtydu and Cei Bach. He built himself a tŷ unnos (*one night house*) – a house erected overnight on common land. If smoke was seen coming from the chimney by daybreak, the owner was deemed to have squatter's rights.

The area was very remote and ideal for smugglers to lie low from the authorities. Siôn Cwilt would get to know whenever a smuggling ship was due to land and would go down to the beach, armed with a pistol and cutlass and with ponies to carry off the contraband. According to tradition many of the gentry in this area relied on Siôn Cwilt for their supplies of wine and spirits, Sir Herbert among them.

The authorities did everything they could to try to catch Siôn Cwilt, but to no avail. Richard Phillips was the salt officer in New Quay at the time, where a riding officer called Joseph Jones was also stationed. Jones had up to seventeen armed men under his command to try to stop the smuggling of salt along the coast. The revenue men had a watch house in New Quay to look out for smuggling ships, and this was also where the chief officer and his family lived. But despite all their efforts, Siôn Cwilt always managed to stay

1. Siôn Cwilt is celebrated in a tavern at New Quay...;
2. ...and in a local school's name!

one step ahead of the authorities and they failed to catch him.

He became quite a folk hero in Ceredigion, but little is known about him because he was too successful. Had he been caught then court transcripts and other reports would provide us with more information.

Thomas Knight

Knight owned a number of armed ships, including one with 24 guns and a crew of forty which operated in the Bristol Channel from his headquarters on Barry Island. He also had a number of fortified bases along the south Wales coast. He would smuggle wines and tobacco from the Channel Islands and soap from Ireland.

In 1783, Knight, described as a 'desperate ruffian', arrived on Barry Island in a brig called the John O Combe, and made it his base for the storing of contraband. Initially, the revenue men did not pay him much attention and with the support of the locals he took advantage of this, making Barry Island a stronghold for his activities. It is said that he had between 60 and 70 men on the island and that the revenue officers could not get any help from the locals, such was Knight's influence in the area. He was a dangerous man, who would not think twice before firing on revenue ships.

Then, in 1784, the revenue service managed to seize a large consignment of Knight's tobacco which was hidden in Goldcliff, but because of the local support for Knight, it was impossible to get any help from anybody in the district and the contraband had to be transported to Cardiff escorted by a contingency of armed men from outside the area.

In the end, following a fierce battle with revenue officers and soldiers, Knight had to flee from the island in 1785 and moved his headquarters to Lundy. However, his successor, William Arthur, proved to be a lot worse.

Barry Island

William Arthur

Arthur, from Pennard on the Gower, became the leader of a large gang of smugglers who operated in the Bristol Channel. He was described in August 1788 by the Swansea Tax Collector as 'a notorious smuggler' and by another as 'the most daring smuggler in Glamorgan during the eighteenth century'. Arthur lived in Great Highway Farm, while his criminal associate, John Griffiths, lived in Little Highway Farm. Both of these farmhouses were used to store illegal goods. In 1786 a dozen revenue men attacked Great Highway farm, but Arthur had been tiped-off that they were on their way and was ready for them – 'a Body of desperate fellows . . . amounted to One hundred'. After a fierce fight, the revenue men had to run for their lives. There were other raids on the farm, twice in 1788 – both unsuccessful.

A story is told in the area about a revenue officer who found a cask of brandy hidden in the attic of one of the Highway farms. He sent for more men to help him while he kept watch on the cask. Downstairs, the smugglers started shouting and singing which masked the sound of a hole being drilled through the ceiling and into the cask, the brandy being emptied into a strategically placed tub downstairs!

Many of the revenue men were afraid of Arthur and they requested a navy ship to be permanently stationed at Penarth and for sixty soldiers to help them take Barry Island. In 1788, the revenue men raided Barry Island twice, but they had to wait until 1791 before they succeeded in driving Arthur from there, a feat that was only achieved with the help of sixty armed dragoons. It is said that the Arthur family moved to Ynystawe, between Clydach and Morriston, where they built a large house called Cwmdwr. In April 1804 his farms on the Gower were raided and illegal goods were found in the cellars. According to the Swansea Tax Collector, 'these farms were supplied many years with foreign spirits and other uncustomed goods to a vast amount'.

One of Arthur's ships was the Cornwall, a pilot boat of about 20 tons which was stationed at Ilfracombe in Devon. A major advantage of using pilot boats was that their work involved going out to meet larger ships which had reached the Bristol Channel, to guide them safely to port. Naturally, this gave the smugglers an excellent opportunity to take goods from these ships before they landed. The Cornwall had been caught several times with illegal goods on board, but every time the captain had a sufficient excuse and was released. Then, in 1783, she was caught with gin and tea onboard and the revenue men this time seized both the ship and the goods.

Arthur subsequently wrote to the revenue service asking them to release his ship as the tea and gin had been placed aboard without the knowledge of the captain or himself. But according to Peter Fosse, the Ilfracombe Tax Collector, the Cornwall had been used 'in an illicit trade between the island of Lundy and the coasts of Cornwall, Devon, Somerset and Wales in the Bristol Channel'. He added that there was 'great reason to think that the seizure of tea and brandy made by the officers here in the month of November last came out of the said boat, as she lay at anchor near the place where the seizure was made'. The revenue service refused Arthur's submission and the Cornwall was sawn into three sections and sold to pay costs and provide a reward for the revenue men.

One of William Arthur's descendants became a vice-admiral in the Royal Navy and Port Arthur in China, or Loushunk'ou as it is called today, was named after him.

Huw Andro

According to tradition, one of the leading smugglers of salt on the Llŷn Peninsula in the eighteenth century was Huw Andro of Llanfaelrhys. Hugh Andrews came originally from Scotland and was washed ashore on Ynys Enlli (*Bardsey Island*) after his ship got into difficulties in a storm. He was the only survivor. He was carried to Rhedynog Goch on the island, where he was looked after by Siân, the farmer's only daughter. On Enlli, not only did he learn to speak Welsh, but he also fell in love with Siân. After they married they moved to Llanfaelrhys on the mainland where Huw was helped by a local ship's carpenter in the building of a fairly large boat which he named Enlli. He would use her for fishing. Also Siân was an expert in the preparation of herbal medicines and Andro and his son, ifan, would sometime cross to Ireland in the Enlli to sell her remedies.

The squire of Bodwrdda soon heard of Andro's trips to Ireland and accused him of smuggling salt. Andro refuted these allegations, but he strongly suspected that the squire knew more about smuggling salt than he let on.

One night Huw spotted a fairly large ship sailing towards Aberdaron. He hurried to the village where he saw a group of men, including the squire, leaving the Ship Inn. The ship landed on the beach and the men proceeded to unload sacks and carry them to the inn.

Huw returned to Aberdaron the following day and sneaked into the cellar where he discovered that the sacks contained salt. Andro now knew that the squire was both a magistrate and a smuggler!

He decided that he himself would now start smuggling salt and sell it to local people at a cheaper price than the squire. Many local people helped him by watching the beaches and warning him if any revenue men were in the vicinity. He would sometimes land his salt in Porth Ysgo, at other times in Porth Cadlan, Porth Meudwy, Porth Ferin, Porthor or on Aberdaron beach itself.

But the squire came to hear of Andro's exploits and informed the revenue service. Huw had been stopped many a time but luckily he had always been able to hide the salt in the myriad caves along the coast.

'Y Cafn' – the landing haven on Bardsey

But one night he was caught whilst landing on Aberdaron beach. The revenue men had been lying in wait in the cellar of the Ship Inn for two days. 'Have you any salt in your boat?' they asked him. 'Yes,' he replied, but as they reached the boat he opened a hatch on the bottom and water poured in washing the salt out.

Not only did Andro keep salt in various caves but he also kept some in the loft of his house. He had warned his children, Ifan and Blodwen, not to tell anyone. But one day, at a hiring fair in Aberdaron, Blodwen fell whilst dancing and hurt her head. She was carried to a nearby farmhouse and when she regained consciousness she thought she was at home and shouted, "Not to the loft!"

One of the squire's men heard this and suspected that this was where Andro kept his salt. He hurried to Bodwrdda, while Andro and his son rushed home. Andro had only seconds to act before the revenue men arrived, but he managed to throw water on the fire, extinguishing it so that it was impossible for the revenue men to see anything. Some of the officers then rushed to the nearby Ysgo farmhouse to light their lanterns and in the confusion Andro had an opportunity to throw the

sacks of salt out of the skylight and move them to a safe place – hiding them later in Llanfaelrhys church. When the revenue men returned with their lanterns and searched the house, there was not a grain of salt to be found.

It is said that Huw Andro once went to Ireland and when his companion went to a house to buy salt, he found there someone who thought that he had been bewitched. The man was told that Huw Andro could cure him. When Huw was called to the house he recited this verse (in Welsh) over the patient as a magic incantation:

> I came here from a far land
> If you don't get worse, I won't make you better
> We'll take a look at Mynydd Rhiw
> I don't care if you live or die.

When he returned to Ireland some time later to get more salt Huw, received a warm welcome from the Irishman who was now completely cured.

Ogof Smyglwyr ('smuggler's cave') at Porthor beach near Aberdaron

This is a poem which used to be recited in Llŷn about Huw Andro:

> The story is to be heard on the lips of the wind
> Above the currents of the coasts of Llŷn,
> Huw Andro is the hero
> Huw Andro the old smuggler
> Who defeated the squire himself.

Catherine Lloyd

Although there were many women who helped to hide illegal goods, there were very few who played a prominent role in the actual smuggling.

Catherine Lloyd was the landlady of the Ferry Inn in Briton Ferry, and she was the leader of a band of local smugglers. It was she who supplied the money to buy the illegal goods and who then stored them in her inn.

During the eighteenth century, coal ships from Neath, trading with Ireland, were often used to bring contraband into the area. In 1726, when revenue men recovered brandy and wine from one of these ships, some of Catherine Lloyd's men seized the goods back, giving a severe beating to the officer guarding them.

By 1730, the inn had changed its name to the Bretton Ferry, while Catherine Lloyd was still the landlord. Then, one day, she made a mistake: 'Edward Dalton . . . Stop'd at the publick house to drink a Pint of ale, the woman of ye house, one CATHERINE LLOYD a widdow not suspecting him to be an officer bro't out the s'd goods and offer'd the same to sale as India Goods, moreover told they were RUN GOODS she had secured the night before . . . Said Widdow is very well to pass in ye world and Suppos'd to have All Her Riches by Running of Goods for SHE is an old offender and NOTED SMUGGLER.'

Smuggling continued in the area for another century, with women still in charge of the illegal trade. In 1758, the Briton Ferry revenue men received a letter naming four women who had travelled from Neath to Bridgwater in Somerset to buy tea for smuggling.

The beach on the estuary at Barmouth

John Jones

John Jones was the captain of the *Catherine*, a 140 ton brigantine from Barmouth, and worked for the merchant David Galway who had centres at Roscoff in Britanny, and Port Rush in Ireland. Galway ran a lucrative business smuggling tobacco to France and brandy from France to Britain. Goods could be brought into various ports, kept in the customs house, and if they were taken out of the country within six months there was no tax to be paid on them. Traders such as Galway were able to take advantage of this because the India Company had a monopoly on tobacco products in France which meant that they were expensive, leading to a considerable amount of smuggling into the country at times. John Jones smuggled tobacco into France and brought illicit brandy back into England and Wales.

On his last voyage he was carrying tobacco from Liverpool to Bayonne and Lorient, but was caught in a violent storm and failed to land his cargo on the beaches. The Catherine had been damaged in the storm and was forced to sail to Lorient. It was there, in June 1791, that John Jones was arrested.

The Witches of Llanddona

Sometime in the eighteenth century, a strange family landed on Llanddona beach at Traeth Coch in Anglesey, in a boat that had neither oars nor a tiller. It is believed that they had been forced to leave Ireland possibly on account of accusations of witchcraft. It is said that they spoke neither Welsh nor English, only Gaelic. They very rarely mixed with the inhabitants of Llanddona and for generations they married within their own family and continued to speak their own language.

Not long after their arrival in Anglesey, the men of the family started helping local smugglers to bring contraband ashore from the Isle of Man, and after they had saved a bit of money they set themselves up as smugglers in their own right. It was not only the locals that feared them; the revenue men were also very wary of going after them. It was believed that if a member of the family was caught, he would release a black fly that he kept in his handkerchief and which would fly straight into the eye of his captor causing permanent damage to that man's sight.

The family were successful smugglers for generations, relying on a combination of fear of their alleged ability to cast spells and their intimate knowledge of the eastern coast of Anglesey to keep the revenue men and everyone else at bay.

The Ship inn at Traeth Coch

Boaz Pritchard

Boaz Pritchard was a successful Caernarfon merchant and grocer who owned a small sloop called the Lively. He used this ship to sail as far as the Channel Islands to buy apples and other goods for his warehouse. But it was not only legal goods that were carried in the Lively, casks of spirits would also be hidden amongst the cargo. Boaz' Brandy became well known throughout the areas around Caernarfon and in Llŷn. However, not every voyage was successful. He was first caught off Porthdinllaen in 1828 and again in 1834, but somehow managed to persuade the authorities to release him each time. He continued with the smuggling, and it is said that he took over six hundred casks of brandy to Ynys Enlli in 1835.

There were rumours in the area, especially in Caernarfon, concerning a ghostly hearse which meandered along the streets in the dead of night. These stories frightened some of the townsfolk. There were those who claimed that if you saw the hearse you would be cursed and that the next corpse to be carried in it would be yours! In reality, it was Boaz Pritchard using a hearse to deliver illegal brandy!

But his smuggling days came to an end in 1838 when he was caught once again off Porthdinllaen, and his ship impounded. When his warehouse in Caernarfon was searched, they found ninety nine casks of brandy, together with the hearse and an empty coffin! As a result, Boaz Pritchard was given a long term in prison as a punishment for all his smuggling.

A love story and a smuggling yarn combined ...

Braich Celyn is one of the oldest houses in Aberdyfi and it is said that one of the most prominent members of the local gentry used to live there at one time, using it as a base for his smuggling activities. Smuggling was so prolific on the shores of the Dyfi that a sloop was sent from London to try to put a stop to it. The sloop came to Aberdyfi and its handsome captain went to look for a particular smuggler and his illegal goods. However it wasn't smuggled goods that he found, but instead a beautiful young girl called Elfrida – the daughter of the suspected smuggler. The two fell in love, meeting frequently on the beach and in the nearby woods.

The handsome captain, however, had not forgotten why he had been sent to Aberdyfi and would often question Elfrida about her father's activities. One night, the captain heard that a Dutch schooner full of illegal spirits was about to arrive in the estuary and he knew that Elfrida's father would soon come down to the beach to collect them. The captain placed his men to watch the path from Braich Celyn to the beach while he went to tell Elfrida that he would soon have to leave the area and if her father were to be arrested then they could never meet again.

Of course Elfrida did not want him to leave and she suggested that if they married she could leave with him. He agreed and a priest was called to Braich Celyn to marry them secretly. But during the ceremony, Elfrida's father and his men came into to the room from a hidden passage that ran down to the beach. They had escaped from the revenue men, and the father was absolutely livid to see his daughter with the captain. He ordered a new wall to be built in one part of the house behind which he imprisoned the newly weds.

To this day, there is a double wall in the house, and people claim that sometimes they can hear the two lovers screaming from behind it. About a century ago, when renovation work was being done on the house, some bones and a gold ring was found behind the wall.

Madam Wen

Einir Wyn came to fame as a character in William D. Owen's exciting novel Madam Wen, in which she is portrayed as a heroine and 'Robin Hood' of Anglesey. It is not known for certain whether there is a historical basis for this story, but recent research has confirmed that the character Einir Wyn was based on Margaret Wynne, the wife of Robert Williams, the squire of Chwaen Wen towards the middle of the eighteenth century. The novel contains a lively account of smuggling activities at that time.

Conclusion

The tradition of smuggling is very old and has changed little in essence over the centuries. It is true to say that some periods have been more active than others, depending on the level and nature of taxation, and that the goods themselves have varied accordingly. There are old stalwarts like booze and 'bacco and many new items like the drugs and fake designer clothes of today. But there is a world of difference between the illicit landing of salt, spirits, tea, tobacco, spices, soap and candles of the eighteenth century as compared to the cocaine, heroin, guns, pornography and human trafficking of today. That is a story in its own right.

Smuggling has always been conducted by those willing to break the law, the extent of which ranges from the small scale personal venture not to declare certain goods when going through customs to large scale importation of illicit materials by international criminal syndicates, old and new.

The success of smuggling during that first 'golden age', over two hundred years ago, was fuelled by public dissatisfaction and reaction against what were seen as oppressive tolls on essential items imposed on the poor by an oppressive and undemocratic government of rich landlords. No unjust law or tax will be respected if it is not acceptable to those whom it affects. That is a lesson which governments need to learn even today.

Sources

Smuggling, A History 1700–1970, D Phillipson, (1973)

Working the Welsh Coast, Mike Smylie, (2005)

Contraband Cargoes, Neville Williams, (1959)

The Compleat Smuggler, J. Jeferson Farjeon, (1938)

Smuggling in Cornwall, Frank Graham, (1964)

Smugglers, Charles G Harper, (1966)

Honest Thieves, the Story of the Smugglers, Patrick Pringle, (1938)

Smuggling in Cornwall and Devon, Lisa Newcombe, (1989)

Smugglers of the Isle of Wight, Richard J Hutchings, (1990)

Welsh Smugglers, K.C. Watkins, (1975)

Scottish Smugglers, Jean Simmons, (1975)

Tales of the Cornish Smugglers, John Vivian

The Smuggling Coast, John A Thompson, (1989)

Cofiant Lewis Morris 1700/1-42, Y Parchedig Dafydd Wyn Wiliam, (1997)

Cofiant William Morris (1705-63), Y Parchedig Dafydd Wyn Wiliam (1995)

William Morris – Swyddog Tollau, Dafydd Wyn Wiliam, Traf. Cymd. Hynafiaethwyr a Naturiaethwyr Môn (1992), tud 63-93

Smuggling on the Exmoor Coast 1680–1850, (2001) John Travis,

Smuggling in Rye and District, Kenneth M. Clark (1977)

Illicit Trading in Wales in the Eighteenth Century, G.I. Hawkes, Maritime Wales, 10, (1986) tud. 89-107

Legal and Illegal Shipping 1660–1786, Aled Eames, Ships and Seamen of Anglesey (1981) tud. 99-132

Smyglo a Helynt y Tollau, David Thomas, Hen Longau Sir Gaernarfon (1952) tud. 68-83

The Smugglers, Timothy Green (1969)

Websites:

A great deal of information can be obtained by googling 'smugglers' eg:
www.wikipedia.com (under 'smugglers')
www.rhiw.com
www.smugglers.com